D0701359

THE OFFICE INBOX

JOKE BOOK

jokes for him

THE OFFICE INBOX

JOKEBOOK

jokes for him

First Edition

Edited by Jane Rooke
Printed in Sydney, Australia

Copyright © 2006

Drum Publishing

ISBN 1921263008

Published in Australia
by Drum Publishing
Erskineville, Sydney

www.drumpublishing.com.au

Text design and typesetting
by Louise Jackson-Moore

Cover image
by Louise Jackson-Moore

Layout & internal illustrations
Xou Pty Ltd
www.xou.com.au

Back cover pixel art from
www.istockphoto.com

Printed in Australia
by Ligare, Sydney

© This book is copyright.
Apart from any fair dealing for the purposes of private study,
research, criticism or review permitted under the *Copyright Act*
of 1968, no part may be stored or reproduced by any
process without prior written permission.
Enquiries should be made to the publisher.

Contents

SUBJECT: ARMY TIME

A crusty old Sergeant Major found himself at a gala event, hosted by a local liberal arts college. There was no shortage of extremely young, idealistic ladies in attendance, one of whom approached the Sergeant Major for conversation.

She said, "Excuse me, Sergeant Major, but you seem to be a very serious man. Is something bothering you?"

"Negative, ma'am," the Sergeant Major said, "Just serious by nature."

"The young lady looked at his awards and decorations and said, "It looks like you have seen a lot of action."

The Sergeant Major's short reply was, "Yes, ma'am, a lot of action."

The young lady, tiring of trying to start up a conversation, said, "You know, you should lighten up a little. Relax and enjoy yourself."

The Sergeant Major just stared at her in his serious manner. Finally the young lady said, "You know, I hope you don't take this the wrong way, but when is the last time you had sex?"

The Sergeant Major looked at her and replied, "1955."

She said, "Well, there you are. You really need to chill out and quit taking everything so seriously! I mean, no sex since 1955!"

She took his hand and led him to a private room where she proceeded to 'relax' him several times.

Afterwards, and panting for breath, she leaned against his bare chest and said, "Wow, you sure didn't forget much since 1955!"

The Sergeant Major, glancing at his watch, said in his matter-of-fact voice, "I hope not, it's only 2130 now."

GOTTA LOVE THAT MILITARY TIME !!!!

SUBJECT: AFL SEASON 2007

Prior Notice ...

It is likely that the AFL competition for 2007 will have to be cancelled.

Under the new Anti Terrorism Laws the Bombers are banned, the new Industrial Relations legislation rules out the Dockers and the Asian Bird flu epidemic is wreaking havoc with the Crows, Eagles, Hawks, Magpies and Swans.

Any transfers to the Kangaroos, Cats, Lions, Dogs and Tigers must now be quarantined for at least 12 months.

Religious vilification laws mean that no one can legally barrack For the Demons or the Saints.

This only leaves the Power and the Blues who no one wants to Barrack for anyway.

SUBJECT: AGEING

I've sure gotten old. I've had two bypass surgeries, a hip replacement, new knees. Fought prostate cancer and diabetes.

I'm half blind, can't hear anything quieter than a jet engine, take 40 different medications that make me dizzy, winded, and subject to blackouts.

Have bouts with dementia.

Have poor circulation, hardly feel my hands and feet any more.

Can't remember if I'm 85 or 92.

Have lost all my friends.

But, thank God, I still have my driver's license.

SUBJECT: AIR TRAFFIC CONTROL CHATTER...

Tower: "Delta 351, you have traffic at ten o'clock, six miles!"
Delta 351: "Give us another hint! We have digital watches!"

Tower: "TWA 2341, for noise abatement turn right 45 Degrees."
TWA 2341: "Centre, we are at 35,000 feet. How much noise can we make up here?"
Tower: "Sir, have you ever heard the noise a 747 makes when it hits a 727?"

From an unknown aircraft waiting in a very long takeoff queue: "I'm f*cking bored!"
Ground Traffic Control: "Last aircraft transmitting, identify yourself immediately!"
Unknown aircraft: "I said I was f...ing bored, not f...ing stupid!"

O'Hare Approach Control to a 747: "United 329 heavy, your traffic is a Fokker, one o'clock, three miles, Eastbound."
United 329: "Approach, I've always wanted to say this... I've got the little Fokker in sight."

SUBJECT: AUSTIN POWERS PICK UP LINES

(Lick finger and wipe on her shirt) Let's get you out of these wet clothes.

Nice legs... what time do they open?

Do you work for UPS? I thought I saw you checking out my package.

You've got 206 bones in your body, want one more?

Can I buy you a drink or do you just want the money?

I may not be the best looking guy here, but I'm the only one talking to you.

I'm a bird watcher and I'm looking for a Big Breasted Bed Thrasher, have you seen one?

I'm fighting the urge to make you the happiest woman on earth tonight.

Wanna play army? I'll lay down and you can blow the hell outta me.

I wish you were a Pony Carousel outside Superdrug, so I could ride you all day long for a quarter.

Oh, I'm sorry, I thought that was a braille name tag.

I'd really like to see how you look when I'm naked.

Is that a ladder in your stockings or the stairway to heaven?

You might not be the best looking girl here, but beauty is only a light switch away.

You must be the limp doctor because I've got a stiffy.

I'd walk a million miles for one of your smiles, and even farther for that thing you do with your tongue.

If it's true that we are what we eat, then I could be you by morning.

I lost my puppy, can you help me find him? I think he went into this cheap motel room.

You know if I were you, I'd have sex with me.

You. Me. Whipped cream. Handcuffs. Any questions?

F*ck me if I'm wrong, but is your name Helga Titsbottom?

My name is (name)... remember that, you'll be screaming it later.

Do you believe in love at first sight or should I walk by again?

Hi, I'm Mr. Right. Someone said you were looking for me.

My friend wants to know if YOU think I'M cute.

Hi, the voices in my head told me to come over and talk to you.

My name isn't Elmo, but you can tickle me any time you want to.

I wish you were a door so I could bang you all day long.

I've lost my phone number, can I have yours?

If you were the last woman and I was the last man on earth, I bet we could do it in public.

Wanna come over for some pizza and sex? No? Why, don't you like pizza?

Baby, I'm an American Express lover... you shouldn't go home without me.

Do you sleep on your stomach? Can I?

Do you wash your pants in Windex because I can see myself in them.

SUBJECT: ARTHRITIS

The drunk smelling like the brewery got on the bus.

He sat next to the local priest. The drunk's shirt was stained, his face full of bright red lipstick and a bottle of rum sticking out of his pocket. Opening his newspaper started to read. A couple of minutes later he asked the priest.

"Father what causes arthritis?"

"Mister it's caused by loose living, being with cheap wicked women, too much alcohol and contempt for his fellow man."

"Well I'll be damned" said the drunk and returned to his paper.

The priest thinking about what he said, turned to the man and apologised.

"I'm sorry, I didn't mean to come on so strong. How long have you had arthritis?"

"I don't Father, I was just reading in the paper that the Pope has it."

SUBJECT: MORE ACCURATE COMPUTER RELATED ACRONYMS

PCMCIA	People Can't Memorise Computer Industry Acronyms.
ISDN	It Still Does Nothing.
APPLE	Arrogance Produces Profit-Losing Entity.
SCSI	System Can't See It.
DOS	Defunct Operating System.
BASIC	Bill's Attempt to Seize Industry Control.
IBM	I Blame Microsoft.
DEC	Do Expect Cuts.
CD-ROM	Consumer Device, Rendered Obsolete in Months.
OS/2	Obsolete Soon, Too.
WWW	World Wide Wait.
MACINTOSH	Most Applications Crash. If Not, The Operating System Hangs.
LOTUS	Lots Of Trouble, Usually Serious.

SUBJECT: THE AMERICAN

An Aussie, a little man, was sitting at a bar in Sydney when this huge, burly American guy walks in. As he passes the Aussie, he hits him on the neck knocking him to the floor. The big, burly Yank says, "That's a karate chop from Korea."

Well, the Aussie gets back on his bar stool and resumes drinking his beer.

The burly Yank then gets up to go to the bathroom and, as he walks by the Aussie, he hits him on the other side of the neck and knocks him to the floor. "That's a judo chop from Japan," he says.

The Aussie decides he's had enough and leaves.

A half hour later he comes back and sees the burly Yank bastard sitting at the bar. He walks up behind him and smacks him on the head, knocking him out. The Aussie says to the bartender, "When he wakes up mate, tell him that was a f*ckin' crowbar from Bunnings."

SUBJECT: ANNIVERSARIES

Three men, a doctor, a lawyer, and a biker, were sitting in a bar talking over a few drinks. After a sip of his martini, the doctor said, "You know, tomorrow is my anniversary. I bought my wife a diamond ring and a new Mercedes. I figure if she doesn't like the diamond ring, then at least she will like the Mercedes, and she will know that I love her."

After finishing his scotch, the lawyer said, "Well, on my last anniversary, I bought my wife a string of pearls and a trip to the Bahamas. I figured if she didn't like the pearls, then at least she would have enjoyed the trip, and she would have known that I loved her."

The Biker then took a big swig from his beer and said, "Yeah, well for my anniversary, I got my old lady a t-shirt and a vibrator. I figured if she didn't like the t-shirt, then she could go f*ck herself."

SUBJECT: AIDS LEAFLET

Dear Sir,
I have just received the Aids Leaflet, through my door, and would like to apply straight away for Aids. I have been on the dole for ten years, and have been living on supplementary benefits, and any other State aid I can get.

It now seems I will be getting aid for sex. It's a pity that this aids has come so late, as I have 15 children and have been wondering if you will be paying for any back payments. Your leaflet states that the more sex I have, the more chance I have of getting Aids. My only problem here is persuading my wife, who is not so keen after 15 kids. Several years ago, I bought some sex aids but she showed little interest, and they were hardly used. Would there be any chance of a refund for the $17.27 I paid for them?

Anyway, I will explain to her that the Government will be now paying us for the sex we have, and I'm sure she will agree that we can't let a chance like that slip away.

You also state that I can pass my Aids on, but as you will understand, with a wife and 15 kids to feed, there won't be much to pass on. If buy chance there is a bit left though, I will pass it on to my mother-in-law, who only has her pension.

I understand, from your letter leaflet, that I can get Aids from a blood transfusion, and I intend to write to my local hospital straight away to see if I can have one. Will the Aids I get from the hospital be deducted from the Aids I get from you? Perhaps you will write and let me know.

I am a firm believer in getting all the Aid from the country I can get, and I am sure you will agree that by my past performance, I do qualify for this one. Can you let me know, as soon as possible, how much I will be paid each time, and will it be weekly or a monthly payment.

Yours truly,
Shamus O'Toole.

P. S. Your advert is great, I certainly won't die of ignorance, I know my rights.

SUBJECT: AUSTRALIAN

We are the people of a free nation of blokes, sheilas and the occasional wanker. We come from many lands (although a few too many of us come from New Zealand), and although we live in the best country in the world, we reserve the right to bitch and moan about it whenever we bloody like. We are one nation but divided into many states.

First, there's Victoria, named after a queen who didn't believe in lesbians. Victoria is the realm of Mossimo turtlenecks, cafe latte, Grand Final Day, and big horse races. Its capital is Melbourne, whose chief marketing pitch is that 'it's liveable'. At least that's what they think. The rest of us think it is too bloody cold and wet.

Next, there's New South Wales, the realm of pastel shorts, macchiato with sugar, thin books read quickly and millions of dancing queens. Its capital Sydney has more queens than any other city in the world and is proud of it. Its mascots are Bondi lifesavers that pull their speedos up their cracks to keep the left and right sides of their brains separate.

Down south, we have Tasmania, a state based on the notion that the family that bonks together stays together. In Tassie, everyone gets an extra chromosome at conception. Maps of the state bring smiles to the sternest faces. It holds the world record for a single mass shooting, which the Yanks can't seem to beat no matter how often they try.

South Australia is the province of half-decent reds, a festival of foreigners and bizarre axe murders. SA is the State of Innovation. Where else can you so effectively re-use country bank vaults and barrels as in Snowtown, just out of Adelaide (also named after a queen). They had the Grand Prix, but lost it when the views of Adelaide sent the Formula One drivers to sleep at the wheel.

Western Australia is too far from anywhere to be relevant. Its main claim to fame is that it doesn't have daylight saving because if it did, all the men would get erections on the bus on the way to work. WA was the last state to stop importing convicts and many of them still work there in the government and business.

The Northern Territory is the red heart of our land. Outback plains, sheep stations the size of Europe, kangaroos, jackaroos, emus,

Uluru, and dusty kids with big smiles. It also has the highest beer consumption of anywhere on the planet and its creek beds have the highest aluminium content of anywhere too. Although the Territory is the centrepiece of our national culture, few of us live there and the rest prefer to fly over it on our way to Bali.

And there's Queensland. While any mention of God seems silly in a document defining a nation of half-arsed sceptics, it is worth noting that God probably made Queensland, as it's beautiful one day and perfect the next. Why he filled it with dick heads remains a mystery.

Oh yes and there's Canberra. The less said the better.

We, the citizens of Oz, are united by highways, whose treacherous twists and turns kill more of us each year than murderers. We are united in our lust for international recognition, so desperate for praise we leap in joy when a rag tag gaggle of corrupt IOC officials tells us Sydney is better than Beijing. We are united by a democracy so flawed that a political party, albeit a redneck gun toting one, can get a million votes and still not win one seat in Federal Parliament. Not that we're whingeing, we leave that to our Pommy immigrants.

We want to make 'no worries mate' our national phrase, 'she'll be right mate' our national attitude and *Waltzing Matilda* our national anthem (so what if it's about a sheep–stealing crim who commits suicide). We love sport so much our newsreaders can read the death toll from a sailing race and still tell us who's winning.

And we're the best in the world at all the sports that count, like cricket, netball, rugby league and union, AFL, roo shooting, two up and horse racing. We also have the biggest rock, the tastiest pies, and the worst dressed Olympians in the known universe. Only in Australia can a pizza delivery get to your house faster than an ambulance. Only in Australia do we have bank doors wide open, no security guards, or cameras but chain the pens to the desk.

Stand proud Aussies – we shoot, we root, we vote. We are girt by sea and pissed by lunchtime. Even though we might seem a racist, closed minded, sports obsessed little people, at least we feel better for it.

I am, you are, we are Australians!

P. S. We also shoot and eat the two animals that are on our National Crest!!!! No other country has this distinction!

SUBJECT: AGEING

25 SIGNS YOU HAVE GROWN UP!

1. Your houseplants are alive, and you can't smoke any of them.
2. Having sex in a twin bed is out of the question.
3. You keep more food than beer in the fridge.
4. 6 a.m. is when you get up, not when you go to bed.
5. You hear your favourite song in an elevator.
6. You watch the Weather Channel.
7. Your friends marry and divorce instead of 'hook up' and 'break up'.
8. You go from 130 days of vacation time to 14.
9. Jeans and a sweater no longer qualify as 'dressed up'.
10. You're the one calling the police because those %&@# kids next door won't turn down the stereo.
11. Older relatives feel comfortable telling sex jokes around you.
12. You don't know what time McDonalds closes any more.
13. Your car insurance goes down and your car payments go up.
14. You feed your dog Science Diet instead of McDonalds leftovers.
15. Sleeping on the couch makes your back hurt.
16. You take naps.
17. Dinner and a movie is the whole date instead of the beginning of one.
18. Eating a basket of chicken wings at 3 a.m. would severely upset, rather than settle, your stomach.
19. You go to the drug store for ibuprofen and Antacid, not condoms and pregnancy tests.
20. A $4 bottle of wine is no longer 'pretty good shit'.
21. You actually eat breakfast food at breakfast time.
22. "I just can't drink the way I used to" replaces "I'm never going to drink that much again."
23. 90 per cent of the time you spend in front of a computer is for real work.
24. You drink at home to save money before going to a bar.
25. When you find out your friend is pregnant you congratulate them instead of asking, "Oh shit?"

Bonus:
You read this entire list looking desperately for one sign that doesn't apply to you and can't find one to save your sorry old arse.

SUBJECT: THE ATHEIST

An atheist was taking a walk through the woods.

"What majestic trees! What powerful rivers! What beautiful animals!" he said to himself.

As he was walking alongside the river he heard a rustling in the bushes behind him. He turned to look. He saw a seven foot grizzly charge towards him. He ran as fast as he could up the path. He looked over his shoulder and saw that the bear was closing in on him. He looked over his shoulder again, and the bear was even closer.

He tripped and fell on the ground. He rolled over to pick himself up but saw the bear right on top of him, reaching for him with his left paw and raising his right paw to strike him.

At that instant the Atheist cried out, "Oh my God!..."

Time stopped. The bear froze. The forest was silent.

As a bright light shone upon the man, a voice came out of the sky, "You deny my existence for all of these years, teach others I don't exist, and even credit creation to a cosmic accident. Do you expect me to help you out of this predicament? Am I to count you as a believer?"

The atheist looked directly into the light, "It would be hypocritical of me to suddenly ask You to treat me as a Christian now, but perhaps could you make the BEAR a Christian?"

"Very well," said the voice.

The light went out. The sounds of the forest resumed. Then the bear dropped his right paw, brought both paws together and bowed his head and spoke, "Lord, bless this food, which I am about to receive from thy bounty through Christ our Lord, Amen."

SUBJECT: AUSSIE BLOKE

On a recent transpacific flight, the plane passes through a severe storm. The turbulence is awful, and things go from bad to worse, and then one of the wings are struck by lightening. One woman in particular loses it. Screaming, she stands up in front of the plane. "I'm too young to die," she wails.

Then she yells, "Well, If I'm going to die, I want my last minutes on earth to be memorable! Is there ANYONE on this plane who can make me feel like a WOMAN?"

For a moment there is silence. Everyone has forgotten his own peril.

They all stare, riveted, at the desperate woman in the front of the plane.

Then an Aussie bloke stands up in the rear of the plane.

He is gorgeous: tall, well built, with sun bleached blonde hair and blue eyes. He starts to walk up the aisle, unbuttoning his shirt.

One button at a time...

No one moves...

Everyone is transfixed...

He removes his shirt...

Muscles ripple across his chest...

She gasps...

He whispers...

"Here ya go luv – iron this and then go get me a beer."

SUBJECT: AT LAST, A BLONDE MALE JOKE!

An Irishman, a Mexican and a blonde guy were doing construction work on scaffolding on the 20th floor of a building. They were eating lunch and the Irishman said, "Corned beef and cabbage! If I get corned beef and cabbage one more time for lunch, I'm going to jump off this building."

The Mexican opened his lunch box and exclaimed, "Burritos again! If I get burritos one more time I'm going to jump off, too."

The blonde opened his lunch and said, "Bologna again! If I get a bologna sandwich one more time, I'm jumping too."

The next day, the Irishman opened his lunch box, saw corned beef and cabbage, and jumped to his death.

The Mexican opened his lunch, saw a burrito, and jumped, too.

The blonde guy opened his lunch, saw the bologna and jumped to his death as well.

At the funeral, the Irishman's wife was weeping. She said, "If I'd known how really tired he was of corned beef and cabbage, I never would have given it to him again!"

The Mexican's wife also wept and said, "I could have given him tacos or enchiladas! I didn't realize he hated burritos so much."

(Oh this is GOOD!)

Everyone turned and stared at the blonde's wife. The blonde's wife said, "Don't look at me. He makes his own lunch."

SUBJECT: A BEAR, A LION A ...

A bear, a Lion and a Chicken meet.

The bear says, "If I roar in the forest, the entire forest is shivering with fear."

The Lion then says, "If I roar in the jungle, the entire jungle is shivering with fear."

But then the Chicken says, "Big fu*king deal, I only have to cough and the entire planet sh*ts itself."

SUBJECT: BOB

Doctor Bob had sex with one of his patients and felt guilty all day long. No matter how much he tried to forget about it, he couldn't.

The guilt and sense of betrayal was overwhelming.

But every once in a while, he'd hear an internal, reassuring voice that said, "Bob, don't worry about it. You aren't the first doctor to sleep with one of their patients and you won't be the last. And you're single, so just let it go..."

But invariably, another voice would bring him back to reality, whispering, "Bob... you're a vet..."

SUBJECT: THE BLONDE YEAR IN REVIEW

The Blonde Year In Review

January   Took her new scarf back to the store because it was too tight.

February   Ordered new drapes for her computer because it had windows.

March   Got excited when she finished a jigsaw puzzle in six months because the box said, "two to four years."

April   Was trapped on an escalator for hours when the power went out.

May   Couldn't make Kool-Aid because eight cups of water wouldn't fit into the little packet.

June   Couldn't learn to water ski because she couldn't find a lake with a slope.

July   After losing in a breast stroke swimming competition, complained to the judges that the other swimmers were using their arms.

August   Told her blonde friend to hurry when trying to get into their locked car using a coat hanger because it was starting to rain and the top was down.

September When asked what the capital of California was: answered, "C".

October   Hates M&Ms because they are so hard to peel.

November   Baked a turkey for four days because the instructions said one hour per pound and she weighed 120.

December   Couldn't call 911 because there was no '11' on any phone button.

SUBJECT: BBC TV BLOOPERS

Michael Buerk watching Phillipa Forrester cuddle up to a male astronomer for warmth during BBC1's UK eclipse coverage remarked, "They seem cold out there, they're rubbing each other and he's only come in his shorts."

Ken Brown commentating on golfer Nick Faldo and his caddie Fanny Sunneson lining-up shots at the Scottish Open, "Some weeks Nick likes to use Fanny, other weeks he prefers to do it by himself."

Mike Hallett discussing missed snooker shots on *Sky Sports*, "Stephen Hendry jumps on Steve Davis's misses every chance he gets."

Jack Burnicle was talking about Colin Edwards' tyre choice on *World Superbike Racing*, "Colin had a hard on in practice earlier, and I bet he wished he had a hard on now."

Chris Tarrant discussing the first *Millionaire* winner Judith Keppel on *This Morning*, "She was practising fastest finger first by herself in bed last night."

Winning Post's Stewart Machin commentating on jockey Tony McCoy's formidable lead, "Tony has a quick look between his legs and likes what he sees."

Ross King discussing relays with champion runner Phil Redmond, "Well Phil, tell us about your amazing third leg."

Cricketer Neil Fairbrother hit a single during a Durham v Lancashire match, inspiring Bobby Simpson to observe, "With his lovely soft hands he just tossed it off."

Clair Frisby talking about a jumbo hot dog on *Look North* said: "There's nothing like a big hot sausage inside you on a cold night like this."

James Allen interviewing Ralf Schumacher at a Grand Prix, asked, "What does it feel like being rammed up the backside by Barrichello?"

Steve Ryder covering the US Masters, "Ballesteros felt much better today after a 69."

The new stand at Doncaster race course took Brough Scott's breath away. "My word," he said. "Look at that magnificent erection."

Willie Carson was telling Claire Balding how jockeys prepare for a big race when he said, "They usually have four or five dreams a night about coming from different positions."

Carenza Lewis about finding food in the Middle Ages on *Time Team Live* said, "You'd eat beaver if you could get it."

US PGA Commentator – "One of the reasons Arnie (Arnold Palmer) is playing so well is that, before each tee shot, his wife takes out his balls and kisses them... Oh my god!!!!! What have I just said?!!!!"

Metro Radio – "Julian Dicks is everywhere. It's like they've got eleven Dicks on the field."

Harry Carpenter at the Oxford-Cambridge boat race 1977 – "Ah, isn't that nice. The wife of the Cambridge President is kissing the Cox of the Oxford crew."

Ted Walsh – Horse Racing Commentator – "This is really a lovely horse. I once rode her mother."

New Zealand Rugby Commentator – "Andrew Mehrtens loves it when Daryl Gibson comes inside of him."

Pat Glenn – Weightlifting commentator – "And this is Gregoriava from Bulgaria. I saw her snatch this morning and it was amazing!"

SUBJECT: BLONDE

"You are suffering from what is technically known as an Electra Complex," the psychiatrist is informing his blonde female patient. "In other words, you are in love with your father."

The blonde breaks down into hysterical sobbing.

"Now, now," comforts the shrink. "It's not all that bad."

"Yes.. (sniff)... yes, it is," the blonde gets out between sobs.

"I have no chance at all... he's a married man!"

SUBJECT: BAD JOKE OF THE DAY

A man walks into a doctor's surgery, with a cucumber up his arse, a carrot in his left ear and a banana in his right nostril.

He asks, "What the f*ck is the matter with me Doc?"

Doc replies, "You're not eating properly."

SUBJECT: BREAST IMPLANTS

A British company is developing computer chips that store music in women's breast implants.

This is a major breakthrough, since women are always complaining about men staring at their breasts and not listening to them.

SUBJECT: BLONDE

A blonde decided to redecorate her bedroom. She wasn't sure how many rolls of wallpaper she would need, but she knew that her blonde friend from next door had recently done the same job and the two rooms were identical in size.

"Buffy," she said, "how many rolls of wallpaper did you buy for your bedroom?"

"Ten," said Buffy.

So the blonde bought the ten rolls of paper and did the job, but she had two rolls leftover.

"Buffy," she said. "I bought ten rolls of wallpaper for the bedroom, but I've got two leftover!"

"Yes," said Buffy. "So did I."

SUBJECT: THE BURGLARY

An old man was a witness in a burglary case in Miami. The defence lawyer asks Sam, "Did you see my client commit this burglary?"

"Yes," said Sam, "I saw him plainly take the goods."

The lawyer asks Sam again, "Sam, this happened at night. Are you sure you saw my client commit this crime?"

"Yes" says Sam, "I saw him do it."

Then the lawyer asks Sam, "listen, you are 80 years old and your eye sight might be failing. Just how far can you see at night?"

He quickly replied, "I can see the moon, how far is that?"

SUBJECT: TOP TEN CHILDREN'S BOOKS NOT RECOMMENDED BY THE NATIONAL LIBRARY ASSOCIATION

10.   Clifford the Big Dog is Put to Sleep

9.   Charles Manson Bedtime Stories

8.   Daddy Loses His Job and Finds the Bottle

7.   Babar becomes a Piano

6.   Controlling the playground: Respect through Fear

5.   Curious George and the High-Voltage Fence

4.   The Boy Who Died from Eating All His Vegetables

3.   Things Rich Kids Have, But You Never Will

2.   Let's draw Betty and Veronica without their clothes on

1.   The Care Bears Maul Some Campers and are Shot Dead

SUBJECT: DOES THE CAP FIT
YOU KNOW YOU'RE A BIKER WHEN...

You bought saddlebags so you can carry more beer.

Your best friends are named after animals.

Your best shoes have steel toes.

You have motorcycle parts in the dishwasher.

Your idea of jewellery is chains and barbed wire.

You can tell what kind of bugs they are by the taste of them.

You're only sunburned on the back of your hands.

You carry a picture of your bike in your wallet.

Any day you ride is a good day.

Your other vehicle is a truck with motorcycle ramps in it.

Your three piece suit is chaps, leather vest and a leather jacket.

Your kids learn to ride on the back of your bike before they can walk.

Your garage has more square footage than your house.

Your coffee table collapses from the weight of motorcycle magazines on it.

You throw a party and more bikes show up than cars.

SUBJECT: BUFFALO THEORY

One afternoon at Cheers. Cliff Clavin was explaining the Buffalo Theory to his buddy Norm.

Here's how it went.

"Well ya see Norm. It's like this... A herd of buffalo can only move as fast as the slowest buffalo. And when the herd is hunted, it is the slowest and weakest ones at the back that are killed first. This is natural selection if good for the herd as a whole, because the general speed and health of the whole group keeps improving by the regular killing of the weakest members."

"In much the same way, the human brain can only operate as fast as the slowest brain cells. Excessive intake of alcohol, as we know, kills brain cells. But naturally, it attacks the slowest and weakest brain cells first. In this way, regular consumption of beer eliminates the weaker brain cells, making the brain a faster and more efficient machine. That's why you always feel smarter after a few beers."

WARNING: The consumption of alcohol may create the illusion that you are tougher, smarter, faster and better looking better than most people.

SUBJECT: BULLSHIT BINGO

Do you keep falling asleep in meetings and seminars?
What about those long and boring conference calls?
Here's a way to change all of that.

1. Before (or during) your next meeting, seminar, or conference
    call, prepare yourself by drawing a square five foot by five
    foot is a good size. Divide the square into columns five across
    and five down, this will give you 25 squares.

2. Write the following words/phrases in each block.
    basically – core competencies – best practice – bottom line –
    revisit – obviously – to tell the truth (or 'the truth is') – 24/7
    – benchmark – value added – pro active – win win – think
    outside the box – essentially – 'hit the nail on the head'
    – 'having said that'– 'Ya know what I'm say'n' – at the end
    of the day – touch base – he goes/she goes – client focus(ed)
    – paradigm – leverage

3. Check off the appropriate block when you hear one of those
    words/phrases.

4. When you get five blocks horizontally, vertically, or
    diagonally, stand up and shout, "Bullshit."

Testimonials:

"I had been in the meeting for only five minutes when I won." **Adam**

"My attention span at meetings has improved dramatically." **Daniel**

"What a gas! Meetings will never be the same for me after
my first win." **Julie**

"The atmosphere was tense in the last process meeting as 14 of us
waited for the fifth box." **Ben**

"The speaker was stunned as eight of us screamed, "Bullshit!" for
the third time in two hours." **Richard**

SUBJECT: CAPTAIN SPEAKING

A plane was taking of from Kennedy Airport.

After it reached the comfortable altitude, the captain made an announcement over the intercom, "Ladies and gentlemen, this is your captain speaking. Welcome to flight 218, non-stop from New York to Los Angeles. The weather ahead is good and therefore we should have a smooth and uneventful flight. Now, please sit back and relax... Oh my God!"

The passengers sat in silence, waiting for terrible news.

Then, the captain came back on the intercom and said, "Ladies and Gentlemen, I am sorry if I scared you earlier, but while I was talking, the flight attendant brought me a cup of coffee and spilled the liquid in my lap. You should see the front of my pants."

A passenger sitting near the cockpit said, "That's nothing, you should see the back of mine."

SUBJECT: THE CHEF

Some time ago, President Clinton was hosting a state dinner when, at the last minute, his regular cook fell ill, and they had to get a replacement on short notice.

The fellow arrived and turned out to be a very grubby-looking man named Jon. The President voiced his concerns to his Chief of Staff but was told that this was the best they could do on such short notice.

Just before the meal, the President noticed the cook sticking his finger in the soup to taste it and again complained to the Chief of Staff, but he was told that this man was supposed to be a very good chef.

The meal went okay, but the President was sure that the soup tasted a little funny. By the time dessert came, he was starting to have stomach cramps and nausea.

It was getting worse and worse until finally the President had to excuse himself from the dinner to look for the bathroom.

Passing through the kitchen, he caught sight of the cook, Jon, scratching his rear end, which made him feel even worse.

By now, the President was desperately ill with violent cramps and was so disorientated that he couldn't remember which door led to the bathroom.

He was on the verge of passing out from the pain when he finally found a door that opened. As he unzipped his trousers and ran in, he realised to his horror that he had stumbled into Monica Lewinsky's office with his trousers around his knees.

As he was just about to pass out, she bent over him and heard the President whisper in a barely audible voice, "Sack my cook."

And that folks is how the whole misunderstanding occurred.

SUBJECT: CONFESSIONS

A man with a nagging secret couldn't keep it any longer. In the confessional he admitted that for years he had been stealing building supplies from the lumber yard where he worked.

"How much material did you take?" his priest asked.

"Enough to build my own house, and enough for my son's house, and houses for our two daughters and our cottage at the lake."

"This is very serious," the priest said. "I shall have to think of a far-reaching penance. Have you ever done a retreat?"

"No, Father, I haven't," the man replied. "But if you can get the plans, I can get the lumber."

The new priest is nervous about hearing confessions, so he asks an older priest to sit in on his sessions. The new priest hears a couple confessions, then the old priest asks him to step out of the confessional for a few suggestions.

The old priest suggests, "Cross you arms over your chest and rub your chin with one hand." The new priest tries this. The old priest suggests, "Try saying things like, 'I see,' 'yes,' 'go on,' 'I understand,' and 'how did you feel about that?'"

The new priest says those things, trying them out. The old priest says, "Now, don't you think that's a little better than slapping your knee and saying 'No shit! What happened next?'"

SUBJECT: CAR PARTS

Nelson Mandela is sitting at home watching TV and drinking a beer when he hears a knock at the door. When he opens it, he is confronted by a little Chinese man, clutching a clip board and yelling, "You Sign! You sign!"

Behind him is an enormous truck full of car exhausts.

Nelson is standing there in complete amazement, when the Chinese man starts to yell louder, "You Sign! You sign!" Nelson says to him, "Look, you've obviously got the wrong man" and shuts the door in his face.

The next day he hears a knock at the door again. When he opens it, the little Chinese man is back with a huge truck of brake pads.

He thrusts his clipboard under Nelson's nose, yelling, "You sign! You sign!" Mr. Mandela is getting a bit hacked off by now, so he pushes the little Chinese man back, shouting, "Look, go away! You've got the wrong man. I don't want them!" Then he slams the door in his face again.

The following day, Nelson is resting, and late in the afternoon, he hears a knock on the door again. On opening the door, there is the same little Chinese man thrusting a clipboard under his nose, shouting, "You sign! You sign!"

Behind him are TWO very large trucks full of car parts. This time Nelson loses his temper completely, he picks up the little man by his shirt front and yells at him, "Look, I don't want these! Do you understand? You must have the wrong name! Who do you want to give these to?"

The little Chinese man looks very puzzled, consults his clipboard, and says, "You not Nissan Main Dealer?

SUBJECT: THE CLOSET

A housewife takes a lover during the day, while her husband is at work. Unbeknownst to the housewife, her nine-year-old son was hiding in the closet. Her husband came home unexpectedly, so she hid her lover in the closet. The boy now has company.

Boy: "Dark in here."

Man: "Yes it is."

Boy: "I have a baseball."

Man: "That's nice."

Boy: "Want to buy it?"

Man: "No thanks."

Boy: "My Dad's outside."

Man: "OK, how much?"

Boy: "$250."

In the next few weeks, it happens again that the Boy and the Mum's lover are in the closet together.

Boy: "Dark in here."

Man: "Yes, it is."

Boy: "I have a baseball glove."

Man: "How much?"

Boy: "$750."

Man: "Fine."

A few days later, the father says to the boy, "Grab your ball and glove. Let's go outside and play catch."

The boy says, "I can't. I sold them."

The father asks, "How much did you sell them for?"

The son says, "$1,000."

The father says, "That's terrible to overcharge your friend like that. That is way more than those two things cost. I'm going to take you to church and make you confess."

They go to church, the father alerts the priest, makes the boy sit in the confessional and closes the door.

The boy says, "Dark in here."

The priest says, "Don't start that shit again."

SUBJECT: COMEBACK

A candidate for state election was doing some door to door campaigning, things were going pretty good, he thought, until he came to the house of a grumpy old man.

After the candidate little speech, the old man said, "Vote for you? Why I'd rather vote for the devil!"

"I fully understand sir" said the candidate. "But in case your friend is not running, may I count on your vote."

SUBJECT: CANNIBALS AT WORK

A big corporation recently hired several cannibals in the interest of cultural diversity. "You are all part of our team now," said the HR rep during the welcoming briefing. "You get all the usual benefits and you can go to the cafeteria for something to eat, but please don't eat any of the other employees."

The cannibals promised they would not. Four weeks later, their boss remarked, "You're all working very hard and I'm satisfied with you. However, one of our shipping clerks has disappeared. Do any of you know what happened to him?" The cannibals all shook their heads no.

After the boss left, the leader of the cannibals said to the others, "Which one of you idiots ate the shipping clerk?"

A hand rose hesitantly, to which the leader of the cannibals continued, "You fool! For four weeks we've been eating managers and no one noticed anything."

"But noooooo, you had to go and eat someone who actually does something."

SUBJECT: CHEER UP!!!

If you think life is bad...

How would you like to be an egg?

You only get laid once.

You only get eaten once.

It takes four minutes to get hard.

Only two minutes to get soft.

You share your box with 11 other guys.

But worst of all...

The only chick that ever sat on your face was your mother!!!

So cheer up, Your life ain't that bad!!!

Pass it around to someone who you feel can use a good lay,
I mean day!!!

SUBJECT: CANBERRA'S BEST?

Prime Minister John Howard, Federal Treasurer Peter Costello, and Industrial Relations Minister Kevin Andrews are flying on the executive airbus to a gathering in Canberra when Howard turns to Costello and says, chuckling,

"You know, I could throw a $1000 bill out the window right now and make someone very happy."

Costello shrugs and replies, "Well, I could throw ten $100 bills out the window and make ten people happy."

Not to be outdone, Andrews says, "Well I could throw a hundred $10 bills out the window and make a hundred people happy."

The pilot rolls his eyes and says to his co-pilot, "Such arrogant arses back there. Hell, I could throw all three of them out the window and make millions of people happy."

SUBJECT: THE CAR

After years of scrimping and saving, a husband told his wife the good news, "Honey, we've finally saved enough money to buy what we started saving for in 1979."

"You mean a brand-new Cadillac?" she asked eagerly.

"No," said the husband, "a 1979 Cadillac."

SUBJECT: CHICKEN SURPRISE

A couple go for a meal at a Chinese restaurant and order the 'Chicken Surprise'. The waiter brings the meal, served in a lidded cast iron pot.

Just as the wife is about to serve herself, the lid of the pot rises slightly and she briefly sees two beady little eyes looking around before the lid slams back down.

"Good grief, did you see that?" she asks her husband.

He hasn't, so she asks him to look in the pot. He reaches for it and again the lid rises, and he sees two little eyes looking around before it slams down.

Rather perturbed, he calls the waiter over, explains what is happening, and demands an explanation.

"Please sir," says the waiter, "what you order?"

The husband replies, "Chicken Surprise."

"Ah... so sorry," says the waiter, "I bring you Peeking Duck"

SUBJECT: CHICKEN SOUP

Joseppi was in the hospital and it was time for lunch.

He looked at his lunch and said, "I don't like chicken soup, bring something else."

The orderly said, "It's good for you, the doctor said you should have it."

Joseppi refused to eat. That night, Joseppi's roommate had bad stomach pain, so the nurses came in to give him an enema. By mistake, they gave the enema to Joseppi. The following week, when he was leaving the hospital, a new patient asked him how he liked the hospital.

Joseppi told him, "Well, the hospital itself is pretty good, but they're very strict about their food. Here's a good tip: when they bring up chicken soup you better eat it, or else they'll come back in the middle of the night and shove it up your arse."

SUBJECT: COMEBACK!!

If you ever testify in court, you might wish you could have been as sharp as this policeman.

He was being cross-examined by a defence attorney during a felony trial. The lawyer was trying to undermine the policeman's credibility...

Q: "Officer – did you see my client fleeing the scene?"
A: "No sir. But I subsequently observed a person matching the description of the offender, running several blocks away."

Q: "Officer – who provided this description?"
A: "The officer who responded to the scene."

Q: "A fellow officer provided the description of this so-called offender. Do you trust your fellow officers?"
A: "Yes, sir. With my life."

Q: "With your life? Let me ask you this then officer. Do you have a room where you change your clothes in preparation for your daily duties?"
A: "Yes sir, we do!"

Q: "And do you have a locker in the room?"
A: "Yes sir, I do."

Q: "And do you have a lock on your locker?"
A: "Yes sir."

Q: "Now why is it, officer, if you trust your fellow officers with your life, you find it necessary to lock your locker in a room you share with these same officers?"
A: "Well you see, sir – we share the building with the court complex, and sometimes lawyers have been known to walk through that room."

The courtroom erupted in laughter, and a prompt recess was called.

(The officer on the stand has been nominated for this year's "Best Comeback Line" – and we think he'll win !!.)

SUBJECT: THE COYOTE

This woman is driving into a small town and slams on the brakes as a coyote runs across the road in front of her.

Just as she regains her wits and gets ready to proceed, a cowboy runs right in front of her and catches the coyote by the hind legs and starts screwing it. She screams and drives into town to find the local law.

She sees the local sheriff's car parked in front of the town bar. "It figures," she says as she storms inside. The first thing she notices is an old, old man with a long white beard sitting in the corner jacking-off. She runs up to the sheriff who's sitting at the bar with his drink.

"What kind of sick town are you running here? I drive into town and almost run over some cowboy sodomising an animal... and then... I come in here... and see this old man in the corner abusing himself in public!"

"Well, ma'am," the sheriff slowly replies, "you don't expect him to catch a coyote at his age, do you?"

SUBJECT: HOW MOSES GOT THE TEN COMMANDMENTS

God went to the Arabs and said, "I have Commandments for you that will make your lives better."

The Arabs asked, "What are Commandments?"
The Lord said, "They are rules for living."
"Can you give us an example?"
"You shall not kill." "Not kill? We're not interested."

So God went to the Blacks and said, "I have Commandments."
The Blacks wanted an example, and the Lord said,
"Honour your Father and Mother."
"Father? We don't know who our fathers are."

Then God went to the Mexicans and said, "I have Commandments."
The Mexicans also wanted an example, and the Lord said,
"You shall not steal."
"Not steal? We're not interested."

So God went to the French and said, "I have Commandments."
The French too wanted an example and the Lord said,
"You shall not commit adultery."
"Not commit adultery? We're not interested."

Finally, God went to the Jews and said, "I have Commandments."
"Commandments?" they said, "How much are they?"
"They're free."
"We'll take ten."

Wel, that ought to offend just about everybody equally.

SUBJECT: CIVIL WAR

Early in the Civil War, when the Union armies were suffering repeated defeats, Abraham Lincoln was discussing the war situation with his cabinet.

"How many men do you estimate are in the Confederate army?" a cabinet member asked.

"About a million and a half," said Lincoln.

"That many?" said another member. "I thought the number was considerably less."

"So did I," said Lincoln, "but every time one of our generals lose a battle, he insists that he was outnumbered three to one – and we have about 500,000 men."

SUBJECT: CREEPY

Abraham Lincoln was elected to Congress in 1846.
John F. Kennedy was elected to Congress in 1946

Abraham Lincoln was elected President in 1860.
John F. Kennedy was elected President in 1960.

Both were particularly concerned with civil rights.
Both wives lost a child while living in the White House.

Both Presidents were shot on a Friday.
Both Presidents were shot in the head.

Now it gets really weird.
Lincoln's secretary was named Kennedy.
Kennedy's secretary was named Lincoln

Both were assassinated by Southerners.
Both were succeeded by Southerners named Johnson.

Andrew Johnson, who succeeded Lincoln, was born 1908.
Lyndon Johnson, who succeeded Kennedy, was born 1908.

John Wilkes Booth, who assassinated Lincoln, was born 1839.
Lee Harvey Oswald, who assassinated Kennedy, was born 1939.

Both assassins were known by their three names.
Both names are composed of fifteen letters.

Now hang onto your seat.
Lincoln was shot at the theatre named 'Ford'
Kennedy was shot in a car called 'Lincoln' made by 'Ford'.

Booth and Oswald were assassinated before their trials.
And here's the kicker.
A week before Lincoln was shot, he was in Monroe, Maryland.
A week before Kennedy was shot, he was in Marilyn Monroe.

Lincoln was shot in a theatre, and the assassin ran to a warehouse.
Kennedy was shot from a warehouse, and the assassin ran to
a theatre.

SUBJECT: NEW MEANINGS FOR THE DICTIONARY

BACHELOR
1. A guy who has avoided the opportunity to make some woman miserable.
2. A guy who is footloose and fiance free.

COMPROMISE
1. An amiable arrangement between husband and wife whereby they agree to let her have her way.

DIPLOMAT
1. A man who can convince his wife she would look fat in a fur coat.

HOUSEWORK
1. What the wife does that nobody notices until she doesn't do it.

HUSBAND
1. A man who gives up the privileges he never realised he had.
2. A person who is the boss of his house and has his wife's permission.

JOINT CHEQUE ACCOUNT
1. A handy little device which permits the wife to beat the husband to the draw.

LOVE
1. An obsessive delusion that is cured by marriage.

MISS
1. A title which we brand unmarried women to indicate that they are in the market.

MISTRESS
1. Something between mister and mattress.

MOTHER-IN-LAW
1. A woman who destroys her son-in-laws peace of mind by giving him a piece of hers.

Mrs.
1.   A job title involving heavy duties, light earnings, and no recognition.

SPOUSE
1.   Someone who will stand by you through all the trouble you wouldn't have had if you'd stayed single in the first place.

WIFE
1.   A mate who is forever complaining about not having anything to wear, at the same time that who complains about not having enough room in closet.

SUBJECT: DELIGHTFULLY DIM

A blonde calls her boyfriend and says, "Please come over here and help me. I have a killer jigsaw puzzle, and I can't figure out how to get it started."

Her boyfriend asks, "What is it supposed to be when it's finished?"

The blonde says, "According to the picture on the box, it's a rooster."

Her boyfriend decides to go over and help with the puzzle.

She lets him in and shows him where she has the puzzle spread all over the table. He studies the pieces for a moment, then looks at the box, then turns to his girlfriend and says, "First of all, no matter what we do, we're not going to be able to assemble these pieces into anything resembling a rooster."

He takes her hand and says, "Second, I want you to relax. Let's have a nice cup of tea, and then..." he sighed, "...let's put all these Corn Flakes back in the box."

SUBJECT: MANS DIARY

Dear Diary,

I never quite figured out why the sexual urges of men and women differ so much. And I never have figured out the whole Venus and Mars thing. I have never figured out why men think with their head and women with their heart.

I have never figured out why the sexual desire gene gets thrown into a state of turmoil, when it hears the words, "I do." One evening last week, my wife and I were getting into bed. Well, the passion starts to heat up, and she eventually says, "I don't feel like it right now. I just want you to hold me." I said, "WHAT????!!!" So she says the words that every husband on the planet dreads to hear, "You must not be in tune with my emotional needs as a woman." I'm thinking, "What was her first clue?" I eventually realised that nothing was going to happen that night so I went to sleep.

The very next day, we went shopping at a big [unnamed] department store... I walked around with her while she tried on three different very expensive outfits. She couldn't decide which one to take, so I told her to take all three. She wanted matching shoes, so I said, "Let's get a pair for each outfit." We went to the jewellery deptartment. where she gets a pair of diamond earrings. Let me tell you... she was so excited. She must have thought I was one wave short of a shipwreck.

I started to think she was testing me because she asked for a tennis bracelet when she doesn't even know how to play tennis. I think I threw her for a loop when I said it was OK. She was almost sexually excited from all of this. You should have seen her face when she said, "I think this is all dear, lets go to the cash register."

I could hardly contain myself when I blurted out, "No, honey. I don't feel like buying all of this stuff right now." You should have seen her face... it went completely blank. Then I said, "Really honey! I just wanted you to HOLD this stuff for a while." And just when she had this look like she was going to kill me, I added, "You must not be in tune with my financial capabilities as a man."

I figure that I won't be having sex again until sometime after the Spring of 2008.

SUBJECT: THE DIVORCE

Mickey and Minnie are getting a divorce and Mickey retains a lawyer to speak for him in court. The big day arrives and Mickey's lawyer rises to address the Judge, "Your honour, Mr. Mouse is seeking a divorce from his wife Minnie on the grounds that she is a very stupid mouse."

Whereupon Mickey jumps up and shouts out, "Your honour. Seek leave to confer with my counsel!"

The lawyer comes over to Mickey, very angry. He whispers, "What's wrong? I only just started."

Mickey whispers back to him, "I didn't tell you she was very stupid, I told you she was f*cking Goofy"

SUBJECT: DOWN ON THE FARM

On the farm lived a chicken and a horse, both loved to play together.

One day, the two were playing, when the horse fell into a bog and began to sink. Scared for his life, the horse whinnied for the chicken to get the farmer for help! Off the chicken ran, back to the farm.

Arriving at the farm, he searched and searched for the farmer, but to no avail, for he was gone to town on the only tractor. Running around he spied the farmers new Harley. Finding the keys in the ignition, the chicken sped off with a length of rope, hoping he still had time to save his friends life.

Back at the bog, the horse surprised, but happy, to see the chicken on the shiny Harley, and he managed to get a hold of the loop of rope the chicken tossed him. After tying the other end to the rear bumper of the farmer's bike, the chicken drove slowly forward and, with the aid of the powerful bike, rescued the horse! Happy and proud, the chicken rode the Harley back to the farmhouse, and the farmer was none the wiser when he returned.

The friendship between the two animals was cemented:
Best Buddies, Best pals.

A few weeks later, the chicken fell into a mud pit, and soon, he too began to sink and cried out to the horse to save his life. The horse thought a moment, walked over, and straddled the large puddle. Looking underneath, he told the chicken grab his hangy-down thing and he would lift him out of the pit. The chicken got a good grip, and the horse pulled him out, saving his life.

The moral to the story............... (yes, there's a moral)

"When you're hung like a horse, you don't need a Harley to pick up chicks.

SUBJECT: THE DEFINITION OF CRICKET

As explained to a foreigner.

You have two sides, one out in the field and one in. Each man that's in the side that's in goes out, and when he's out he comes in and the next man goes in until he's out.

When they are all out, the side that's out comes in and the side that's been in goes out and then tries to get those coming in, out. Sometimes you get men still in and not out.

When a man goes out to go in, the men who are out try to get him out, and when he is out he goes in and the next man goes out and goes in.

There are two men called Umpires who stay out all the time and they decide when the men who are in are out.

When both sides have been in and all the men have been out, and both sides have been out twice after all the men have been in, including those who are not out, this is the end of the game.

Simple.

SUBJECT: POOR DAVE

Dave works hard at the plant and spends two nights each week bowling and plays golf every Saturday.

His wife thinks he's pushing himself too hard, so for his birthday she takes him to a local strip club.

The doorman at the club greets them and says, "Hey, Dave! How ya doin'?" His wife is puzzled and asks if he's been to this club before.

"Oh no," says Dave. "He's on my bowling team."

When they are seated, a waitress asks Dave if he'd like his usual and brings over a Budweiser.

His wife is becoming increasingly uncomfortable and says, "How did she know that you drink Budweiser?"

"I recognize her, she's the waitress from the golf club. I always have a Bud at the end of the first nine, honey."

A stripper then comes over to their table, throws her arms around Dave, starts to rub herself all over him and says, "Hi Davey. Want your usual table dance, big boy?"

Dave's wife, now furious, grabs her purse and storms out of the club.

Dave follows and spots her getting into a cab. Before she can slam the door, he jumps in beside her.

Dave tries desperately to explain how the stripper must have mistaken him for someone else, but his wife is having none of it. She is screaming at him at the top of her lungs, calling him every four letter word in the book.

The cabby turns around and says, "Geez Dave, you picked up a real bitch this time."

SUBJECT: DRIVING IN CALIFORNIA

LIFE IN SOUTHERN CALIFORNIA
San Diego, California.

A Highway Patrolman pulled a car over and told the driver that because he had been wearing his seat belt, he had just won $5,000 in the state-wide safety competition.

"What are you going to do with the money?" asked the policeman.

"Well, I guess I'm going to get a driver's license," he answered.

"Oh, don't listen to him," yelled a woman in the passenger seat. "He's a smart aleck when he's drunk."

This woke up the guy in the back seat who took one look at the cop and moaned, "I knew we wouldn't get far in a stolen car."

At that moment, there was a knock from the trunk and a voice said, in Spanish, "Are we over the border yet?"

SUBJECT: THE DOCTOR

A woman from Alabama, who knew absolutely nothing about sex, fell in love with a man and agreed to marry him. As their wedding day approached, she became very nervous about her impending deflowering. Putting her anxiety aside, she decided that she would just marry her man and let him do whatever it was that he wanted to do.

The honeymoon went well and was great fun, but as soon as she got home, she went to see her doctor to question him on some of the new things she'd seen.

"What can I help you with?" he asked.

She said, "Well first, what is that thing between my husband's legs called?"

"Ma'am," he answered, "that there is called a penis."

"I see," she said. "Now what is the big thing on the end of the penis called?"

The old doctor smiled and said, "Why that there is called the head of the penis."

"I do declare!" exclaimed the young woman. "One last question doctor, what are those two big round things about 12-14 inches behind the head of the penis?"

He paused and said, "I'm not sure about your husband, ma'am, but on me, they're called the cheeks of my arse."

SUBJECT: DICTIONARY FOR DECODING PERSONAL ADDS.

WOMEN'S...

40-ish	49
Adventurous	Slept with everyone.
Athletic	No Breasts.
Average Looking	Mooooooooooooooooooo
Beautiful	Pathological Liar.
Emotionally Secure	On Medication.
Feminist	Fat.
Friendship First	Reformed Bitch.
New-Age	Body Hair In Wrong Places.
Open Minded	Desperate.
Outgoing	Loud and Embarrassing.
Professional	Bitch.
Voluptuous	Very Fat.
Large Frame	Hugely fat.
Wants Soul Mate	Stalker.

MEN'S...

40-ish	59
Adventurous	Slept with everything (including the neighbours dog and my ex wife's shower cap.
Athletic	I spend three hours a day in front of a mirror flexing my non biceps and twitching my boobs 'pecks' along to various Tom Jones tunes.
Average Looking	Danny Devito's body with Woody Allen's face.
Handsome	Personal add was written by mother.
Emotionally Secure	Still Married.
In Favour of Women's Rights	Pathological Liar.
Free Spirit	Open relationships wanted.
Friendship First	Small penis.
New-Age	I'll try anything.
Old-Fashioned	Male chauvinist pig.
Open Minded	Any age/any sex.
Outgoing	I will talk/drink/shag anyone under the table.
Professional	Toff.
Cuddly	Beer belly.
Large Frame	Bed bound.
Wants Soul Mate	Middle aged virgin.

SUBJECT: DRIVING

This morning on the expressway, I looked over to my left and there was a woman in a brand new Cruiser, doing 100 miles per hour, with her face up next to her rear view mirror, putting on her eyeliner.

I looked away for a couple of seconds, and then when I looked back she was half way over in my lane, still working on her make up.

As a man I don't scare easily, but she scared me so much I dropped my electric shaver, which knocked the doughnut out of my other hand.

In all the confusion of trying to straighten out the car using my knees against the steering wheel, it knocked my phone mobile phone away from my ear, which fell into the coffee between my legs, splashed, and burned Big Jim and the twins, ruined the damn phone, soaked my trousers, and disconnected an important call.

Damn Women drivers!

SUBJECT: THE DRUNK

A man and his wife are awakened, at three o'clock in the morning by a loud pounding on the door.

The man gets up and goes to the door where a drunken stranger, standing in the pouring rain, is asking for a push.

"Not a chance," says the husband, "it is three o'clock in the morning!"

He slams the door and returns to bed.

"Who was that?" asked his wife.

"Just some drunk guy asking for a push," he answers.

"Did you help him?" she asks.

"No, I did not, it is three o'clock in the morning and it is pouring out there!"

"Well, you have a short memory," says his wife.

"Can't you remember, about three months ago when we broke down, and those two guys helped us? I think you should help him, and you should be ashamed of yourself!"

The man does as he is told, gets dressed, and goes out into the pounding rain.

He calls out into the dark, "Hello, are you still there?"

"Yes" comes back the answer.

"Do you still need a push?" calls out the husband.

"Yes, please!" comes the reply from the dark.

"Where are you?" asks the husband.

"Over here on the swing!" replies the drunk.

SUBJECT: DICK AND GEORGE

One morning Dick Cheney and George W. Bush were having brunch at a restaurant. The attractive waitress asks Cheney what he would like and he replies, "I'll have a bowl of oatmeal and some fruit."

"And what can I get for you, sir?" she asks George W. Bush replies, "How about a quickie?"

"Why, Mr. President," the waitress says, "How rude. You're starting to act like Mr. Clinton and you haven't even been in office for a second term yet!"

As the waitress storms away, Cheney leans over to Bush and whispers, "It's pronounced 'quiche'."

SUBJECT: ENJOYING MARRIAGE

A couple lying in bed. The man says, "I'm going to make you the happiest woman in the world."
The woman replies, "I'll miss you..............................."

"It's just too hot to wear clothes today," Jack says as he stepped out of the shower,
"Honey what do you think the neighbors, would think if I mowed the lawn like this?"
"Probably that I married you for your money," she replied.

He said "shall we try swapping positions tonight sweetheart."
She said that's a good idea...........you stand by the ironing board, and I'll sit on the lounge and fart.

One day my housework-challenged husband decided to wash his sweatshirt. Seconds after he stepped into the laundry, he shouted to me, "What setting do I use on the washing machine?"
"It depends," I replied. "What does it say on your shirt?"
He yelled back "Southern Cross University."
And they say blondes are dumb.

SUBJECT: THE EXCURSION

A group of third, fourth and fifth graders, accompanied by two female teachers, went on a field trip to the local racetrack to learn about commerce, thoroughbred horses and the supporting industry, but mostly just to see the horses.

When it was time to take the children to the bathroom, it was decided that the girls would go with one teacher and the boys with the other.

The teacher assigned to the boys was waiting outside the men's room when one of the boys came out and told her that none of them could reach the urinals.

Having no choice, she went inside, helped the boys with their pants, and began hoisting the little boys up one by one, holding onto their 'wee wees' to direct the flow away from their clothes.

As she lifted one, she couldn't help but notice that he was unusually well endowed. Trying not to show that she was staring, the teacher said, "You must be in the fifth grade, huh?"

"No ma'am," he replied, "I'm the jockey riding Silver Arrow in the seventh!"

SUBJECT: THE EXAMINATION

A young clergyman, fresh out of seminary, thought it would help him better understand the fears and temptations his future congregations faced, if he first took a job as a policeman for several months.

He passed the physical examination. Then came the oral exam to test his ability to act quickly and wisely in an emergency.

Among other questions he was asked, "What would you do to disperse a frenzied crowd?"

He thought for a moment and then said, "I would take up a collection."

SUBJECT: EXTRAORDINARY SIGNS

Bangkok Dry Cleaners
DROP YOUR TROUSERS HERE FOR BEST RESULTS

Hong Kong Tailors
LADIES MAY HAVE A FIT UPSTAIRS

Bucharest Hotel
THE LIFT IS BEING FIXED FOR NEXT DAY. DURING THAT TIME WE REGRET THAT YOU WILL BE UNBEARABLE.

SUBJECT: ENGINEERS

Bubba and Ray (Arkansas mechanical engineers) were standing at the base of a flagpole, looking up. Sandy walked by and asked what they were doing.

"We're supposed to find the height of the flagpole," said Bubba, "but we don't have a ladder."

Sandy took a wrench from her purse, loosened a few bolts, and laid the pole down. Then she took a tape measure from her pocket, took a measurement, announced, "Eighteen feet, six inches," and walked away.

Ray shook his head and laughed. "Ain't that just like a blonde! We ask for the height and she gives us the length!"

SUBJECT: EXPLANATIONS FROM CHAUVINISTS

Q: How many male chauvinists does it take to change a light bulb?
A: None: let her do the dishes in the dark.

Q: What is love?
A: The delusion that one woman varies from another.

Q: What is the differencce between your wife and your job?
A: After five years your job still sucks.

SUBJECT: EMERGENCY...
THESE ARE REAL 911 CALLS!

Dispatcher: 9-1-1 What is your emergency?
Caller: Someone broke into my house and took a bite out of my ham and cheese sandwich.
Dispatcher: Excuse me?
Caller: I made a ham and cheese sandwich and left it on the kitchen table and when I came back from the bathroom, someone had taken a bite out of it.
Dispatcher: Was anything else taken?
Caller: No, but this has happened to me before and I'm sick and tired of it!

Dispatcher: 9-1-1 What is the nature of your emergency?
Caller: I'm trying to reach nine eleven but my phone doesn't have an eleven on it.
Dispatcher: This is nine eleven.
Caller: I thought you just said it was nine-one-one
Dispatcher: Yes, ma'am nine-one-one and nine-eleven are the same thing.
Caller: Honey, I may be old, but I'm not stupid.

Dispatcher: 9-1-1 What's the nature of your emergency?
Caller: My wife is pregnant and her contractions are only two minutes apart
Dispatcher: Is this her first child?
Caller: No, you idiot! This is her husband!

And the winner is...

Dispatcher: 9-1-1
Caller: Yeah, I'm having trouble breathing. I'm all out of breath. Darn... I think I'm going to pass out.
Dispatcher: Sir, where are you calling from?
Caller: I'm at a pay phone. North and Foster.
Dispatcher: Sir, an ambulance is on the way. Are you an asthmatic?
Caller: No
Dispatcher: What were you doing before you started having trouble breathing?
Caller: Running from the police.

SUBJECT: AUSTRALIAN ETIQUETTE

IN GENERAL
1. Never take an open stubby to a job interview.
2. Always identify people in your paddocks before shooting at them.
3. It's tacky to take an esky to church.
4. If you have to vacuum the bed, it's time to change the sheets.
5. Even if you're certain you're included in the will, it's rude to take your ute and trailer to the funeral.

DINING OUT
1. When decanting wine from the box, tilt the paper cup and pour slowly so as not to bruise the wine.
2. If drinking directly from the bottle, hold it with only one hand.

ENTERTAINING IN YOUR HOME
1. A centrepiece for the table should never be anything prepared by a taxidermist.
2. Don't allow the dog to eat at the table, no matter how good his manners.

PERSONAL HYGIENE
1. While ears need to be cleaned regularly, this should be done in private, using one's OWN ute keys.
2. Even if you live alone, deodorant isn't a waste of money.
3. Extensive use of deodorant can only delay bathing by a few days.
4. Dirt and grease under the fingernails is a no-no, it alters the taste of finger foods and if you are a woman it can draw attention away from your jewellery.

DATING
1. Always offer to bait your date's hook – especially on the first date.
2. Be assertive. Let her know you're interested, "I've been wanting to go out with you ever since I read that stuff on the dunny door two years ago."
3. Establish with her parents what time she's expected back. Some will say 11 p.m. others might say, "Monday." If the latter is the answer, it's the man's responsibility to get her to school on time.

CINEMA ETIQUETTE

1. Crying babies should be taken to the lobby and picked up after the movie ends.
2. Refrain from yelling abuse at characters on the screen. Tests have proven they can't hear you.

WEDDINGS

1. Livestock is a poor choice for a wedding gift.
2. Kissing the bride for more than five seconds may cause a drop in your popularity (Excessive use of the tongue is also considered out of place).
3. For the groom, at least, rent a tux. A tracksuit with a cummerbund and a clean football jumper can create a tacky appearance.
4. Though uncomfortable, say, "Yes" to socks and shoes for the occasion.

DRIVING ETIQUETTE

1. Dim your headlights for approaching vehicles, even if your gun's loaded and the roo's in your rifle sight.
2. When entering a roundabout, the vehicle with the largest roo bar doesn't always have the right of way.
3. Never tow another car using pantihose and duct tape
4. When sending your wife down the road with a petrol can, it's impolite to ask her to bring back beer too.

SUBJECT: THE EX

A guy calls up his ex-wife and, disguising his voice, asks to speak to himself.

"Sorry, he doesn't live here any more, we're divorced!"

Next day, the guy does the same thing with the same results.

He does this everyday for a week, and finally his ex-wife realises who it is that keeps calling.

"Look, Bozo! We're divorced! Finito! End of story! When are you going to get that through your fat head?"

"Oh, I know," he replied. "I just can't hear it enough."

SUBJECT: EXAMPLES OF LAWS FOR WHEN MEN RULE THE WORLD

* Looking at your watch and nodding is an acceptance response to I love you.

* The only show opposite Friday night football, would be Friday night football from another angle.

* The funniest guy in the office would get to be the big boss.

* The victors in the athletic competition would killl and eat the losers.

SUBJECT: THESE JUST IN... FACTS

Mosquito repellents don't repel. They hide you. The spray blocks the mosquito's sensors so they don't know you're there.

Dentists have recommended that a toothbrush be kept at least six feet away from a toilet to avoid airborne particles resulting from the flush.

The liquid inside young coconuts can be used as substitute for blood plasma.

No piece of paper can be folded in half more than seven times.

Donkeys kill more people annually than plane crashes.

You burn more calories sleeping than you do watching television.

Oak trees do not produce acorns until they are fifty years of age or older.

The first product to have a bar code was Wrigley's gum.

The king of hearts is the only king without a moustache.

A Boeing 747's wingspan is longer than the Wright brother's first flight.

American Airlines saved $40,000 in 1987 by eliminating one olive from each salad served in first class.

Venus is the only planet that rotates clockwise.

Apples, not caffeine, are more efficient at waking you up in the morning.

The plastic things on the end of shoelaces are called aglets.

Most dust particles in your house are made from dead skin.

The first owner of the Marlboro Company died of lung cancer.

continued...

Michael Jordan makes more money from Nike annually than all of the Nike factory workers in Malaysia combined.

Marilyn Monroe had six toes.

All US Presidents have worn glasses. Some just didn't like being seen wearing them in public.

Walt Disney was afraid of mice.

Pearls melt in vinegar.

Thirty–five percent of the people who use personal ads for dating are already married.

It is possible to lead a cow upstairs... but not downstairs.

A duck's quack doesn't echo, and no one knows why.

The reason fire houses have circular stairways is from the days when the engines were pulled by horses. The horses were stabled on the ground floor and figured out how to walk up straight staircases.

Richard Millhouse Nixon was the first US president whose name contains all the letters from the word, "criminal." The second was William Jefferson Clinton.

Turtles can breathe through their butts.

Butterflies taste with their feet.

In ten minutes, a hurricane releases more energy than all of the world's nuclear weapons combined.

On average, 100 people choke to death on ball–point pens every year.

On average people fear spiders more than death.

Ninety percent of New York City cabbies are recently arrived immigrants.
Elephants are the only animals that can't jump.

Only one person in two billion will live to be 116 or older.

Women blink nearly twice as much as men.

It's physically impossible for you to lick your elbow, (go on try it).

The Main Library at Indiana University sinks over an inch every year because when it was built, engineers failed to take into account the weight of all the books that would occupy the building.

A snail can sleep for three years.

No word in the English language rhymes with 'MONTH.

Average life span of a major league baseball: seven pitches.

Our eyes are always the same size from birth, but our nose and ears never stop growing. SCARY!!!

The electric chair was invented by a dentist.

All polar bears are left handed.

In ancient Egypt, priests plucked EVERY hair from their bodies, including their eyebrows and eyelashes.

An ostrich's eye is bigger than its brain.

TYPEWRITER is the longest word that can be made using the letters only on one row of the keyboard.

"Go," is the shortest complete sentence in the English language.

If Barbie were life size, her measurements would be 39-23-33. She would stand seven feet, two inches tall. Barbie's full name is Barbara Millicent Roberts.

A crocodile cannot stick its tongue out.

The cigarette lighter was invented before the match.

Americans on average eat 18 acres of pizza every day.

SUBJECT: THE FROG

A guy is 67 years old and loves to fish. He was sitting in his boat the other day when he heard a voice say, "Pick me up."

He looked around and could not see any one. He thought he was dreaming when he heard the voice again, "Pick me up."

He looked in the water and there floating on the top was a frog. The man said, "Are you talking to me?"

The frog said, "Yes, I'm talking to you. Pick me up. Then, kiss me and I'll turn into the most beautiful woman you have ever seen. I'll then give you more sexual pleasure that you have ever could have dreamed of."

The man looked at the frog for a short time, reached over, picked it up carefully, and placed it in his front breast pocket. Then the frog said, "What are you nuts, didn't you hear what I said? I said kiss me and I will give you sexual pleasures like you have never had."

He opened his pocket, looked at the frog and said, "Naah, at my age I'd rather have a talking frog."

SUBJECT: FATHOM THIS

A man will pay $2 for a $1 item he needs.

A woman will pay $1 for a $2 item she doesn't need.

SUBJECT: FOOTBALL

The new Liverpool manager sent scouts out around the world looking for a new striker to replace Michael Owen and hopefully win Liverpool the title.

One of the scouts informs him of a young Iraqi striker who he thinks will turn out to be a true superstar. The Liverpool manager flies to Baghdad to watch him and is suitably impressed and arranges him to come over to Anfield. Two weeks later Liverpool are four-nil down to Man Utd only 20 minutes left. The manager gives the young Iraqi striker the nod and on he goes.

The lad is a sensation, scores five in 20 minutes and wins the game for Liverpool. The fans are delighted, the players and coaches are delighted and the media love the new star.

When the player comes off the pitch he phones his Mum to tell her about his first day in English football. "Hello Mum, guess what?" he says. "I played for 20 minutes today, we were four-nil down but I scored five and we won. Everybody loves me, the fans, the media, they all love me."

"Wonderful," says his Mum, "Let me tell you about my day. Your father got shot in the street, your sister and I were ambushed and beaten and your brother has joined a gang of looters, while you were having a great time."

"Sorry?!!" says his Mum, "It's your fault we moved to Liverpool in the first place!"

SUBJECT: FAMILY

A new police recruit was asked what he would do if he had to arrest his own mother.

His answer was, "Call for back up."

SUBJECT: MORE FACTS...

Many years ago in Scotland, a new game was invented.
It was ruled, "Gentlemen Only... Ladies Forbidden" and thus the word GOLF entered into the English language.

In the 1400s a law was set forth that a man was not allowed to beat his wife with a stick no thicker than his thumb. Hence we have 'the rule of thumb'.

The first couple to be shown in bed together on prime time TV were Fred and Wilma Flintstone.

Every day more money is printed for Monopoly than the US Treasury.

Men can read smaller print than women can. Women can hear better.

Coca-Cola was originally green.

The percentage of Africa that is wilderness: 28 per cent
(now get this...)
The percentage of North America that is wilderness: 38 per cent.

The cost of raising a medium size dog to the age of eleven: $6,400.

Intelligent people have more zinc and copper in their hair.

The first novel written on a typewriter: Tom Sawyer.

The San Francisco Cable cars are the only mobile National Monuments.

Each king in a deck of playing cards represents a great king from history:
        Spades – King David
        Hearts – Charlemagne
        Clubs – Alexander, the Great
        Diamonds – Julius Caesar

$$111,111,111 \times 111,111,111 = 12,345,678,987,654,321$$

If a statue in the park of a person on a horse has both front legs in the air, the person died in battle. If the horse has one front leg in the air the person died as a result of wounds received in battle. If the horse has all four legs on the ground, the person died of natural causes.

In English pubs, ale is ordered by pints and quarts... So in old England, when customers got unruly, the bartender would yell at them, "Mind your pints and quarts, and settle down."
It's where we get the phrase, "mind your P's and Q's"

Many years ago in England, pub frequenters had a whistle baked into the rim, or handle, of their ceramic cups. When they needed a refill, they used the whistle to get some service. "Wet your whistle" is the phrase inspired by this practice.

SUBJECT: MAN FACTS

1. Don't trust anything that bleeds for five days and doesn't die.

2. 24 hours in a day, 24 cans in a carton.

SUBJECT: THE FERRARI

A young man goes to buy the best car on the market, a brand new Ferrari GT. It is also the most expensive car in the world, and it costs him $500,000. He takes it out for a spin and stops at a red light.

An old man on a moped, looking about 100 years old, pulls up next to him. The old man looks over at the sleek, shiny car and asks, "What kind of car ya' got there sonny?"

The young man replies, "A Ferrari GTO. It cost half a million dollars!" "That's a lot of money," says the old man. "Why does it cost so much?" "Because this car can do up to 320 miles an hour!" he states proudly. The old moped driver asks, "Mind if I take a look inside?" "No problem," replies the owner. So the old man pokes his head in the window and looks around.

Then, sitting back on his moped, the old man says, "That's a pretty nice car, all right... but I'll stick with my moped!" Just then the light changes, so the young guy decides to show the old man what his car can do. He floors it, and within 30 seconds, the speedometer reads 160 miles per hour.

Suddenly, he notices a dot in his rear view mirror. It seems to be getting closer! He slows down to see what it could be and suddenly

Whoosh! Something whips by him going much faster!

"What on earth could be going faster than my Ferrari?" the young man asks himself. He floors the accelerator and takes the Ferrari up to 250 miles per hour. Then, up ahead of him, he sees that it's the old man on the moped!

Amazed that the moped could pass his Ferrari, he gives it more gas and passes the moped at 275 miles per hour. WHOOOOOOOSHHHHH! He's feeling pretty good until he looks in his mirror and sees the old man gaining on him, AGAIN!

Astounded by the speed of this old guy, he floors the gas pedal and takes the Ferrari all the way up to 320 miles per hour. Not ten seconds later, he sees the moped bearing down on him again! The Ferrari is flat out, and there's nothing he can do! Suddenly, the moped ploughs into the back of his Ferrari, demolishing the rear end. The young man stops and jumps out, unbelievably the old man is still alive! He runs up to the mangled old man and says, "Oh My God! Is there anything I can do for you?"

The old man whispers...

"UN-HOOK... MY... SUSPENDERS... FROM... YOUR... SIDE VIEW... MIRROR!"

SUBJECT: THE FART...

It takes little strain and no art,

To bang out an echoing fart.

The reaction is hearty,

When you fart at a party,

But the sensitive persons depart.

SUBJECT: FUNNY HA HA!

Q: How do you find a blind man in a nudist colony?
A: It's not hard

SUBJECT: FLIGHT ATTENDANT

A chap, sitting in the bar at Melbourne Airport, noticed a very beautiful woman sitting next to him.

He thought to himself, "Wow, she's so gorgeous she must be a flight attendant. I wonder which airline she works for?"

Hoping to pick her up, he leaned towards her and uttered the Delta slogan, "love to fly and it shows?"

She gave him a blank, confused stare and he immediately thought to himself, "Oh crap, she obviously doesn't work for Delta"

A moment later, another slogan popped into his head.
He leaned towards her again, "Something special in the air?"

She gave him the same confused look. He mentally kicked himself, and scratched Singapore Airlines off the list.

Next he tried the Thai Airways slogan, "Smooth as silk?"

This time the woman turned on him
"Exactly what the f*ck do you want?"

The man smiled, slumped back in his chair, and said,
"Ahhhhh, Jetstar!"

SUBJECT: FORESIGHT

A wise school teacher sent a note home to all his pupils' parents on the first day of term. It said, "If you promise not to believe eveything your child says happens at school, I promise not to believe everything they say happens at home."

SUBJECT: FLIGHT TO LONDON

The flight to London was all going well, every one settled in when a blonde in economy class walks up to first class section and sits down.

The flight attendant watches her do this and asks to see her ticket. She then tells the blonde that she paid for economy class and would have to sit in the back.

The blonde replies, "I'm blonde I'm beautiful, I'm going to London and I'm staying right here."

The flight attendant goes to the cockpit and tells the pilot and the co-pilot that there is a blonde bimbo sitting in first class and that she belongs in economy and won't move back to her seat.

The co-pilot goes back to the blonde and tries to explain that because she only paid for an economy she will have to leave and return to her seat.

The blonde replies, "I'm blonde, I'm beautiful, I'm going to London and I'm staying right here."

The co-pilot tells the pilot that he probably should have the police waiting when they land to arrest this blonde woman who won't listen to reason.

The pilot says, "You say she is blonde? I'll handle this. I'm married to a blonde. I speak blonde."

The pilot then goes and whispers in the blondes ear, "Oh I'm sorry" says the blonde and then goes back to her seat in economy.

The flight attendant and co-pilot were amazed, asking the pilot what was whispered to make her move back to her seat without any fuss.

"I simply told her first class isn't going to London."

SUBJECT: FISHING STORY!

At a senior citizen's luncheon, an elderly gentleman and an elderly lady struck up a conversation and discovered that they both loved to fish.

Since both of them were widowed, they decided to go fishing together the next day.

The gentleman picked the lady up, and they headed to the river to his fishing boat and started out on their adventure.

They were riding down the river when there was a fork in the river, and the gentleman asked the lady, "Do you want to go up or down?"

All of a sudden the lady stripped off her shirt and pants and made mad passionate love to the man right there in the boat.

When they finished, the man couldn't believe what had just happened, but he had just experienced the best sex that he'd had in years.

They fished for a while and continued on down the river, when soon they came upon another fork in the river.

He again asked the lady, "Up or down ?"

There she went again, stripped off her clothes, and made wild passionate love to him again.

This really impressed the elderly gentleman, so he asked her to go fishing again the next day.

She said yes and there they were the next day, riding in the boat when they came upon the fork in river, and the elderly gentleman asked, "Up or down ?"

The woman replied, "Down."

A little puzzled and disappointed, the gentleman guided the boat down the river when he came upon another fork in the river and he asked the lady, "Up or down ?"

She replied, "Up."

This really confused the gentleman so he asked, "What's the deal? Yesterday, every time I asked you if you wanted to go up or down you made passionate love to me. Now today, nothing!"

She replied, "Well, yesterday I wasn't wearing my hearing aid and I thought the choices were f*ck or drown."

SUBJECT: GAY FACTS

1. You can kill anyone Honey, including pets.

2. You know someone who was in the emergency room with Richard Gere and the gerbil.

3. You can be in a night club the size of two football fields and still spot the toupee.

4. You only wear polyester when you mean to.

5. You know that being called a 'cheap slut' isn't an insult.

6. You never hold a grudge for longer than a decade or two.

7. You worry about people you don't even know like Kylie Minogue.

SUBJECT: FAMOUS CHINESE DETECTIVE

A man suspected his wife of adultry, so he hired a famouse Chinese detective to spy on her. A few days later he received to report.

Most Hon'rable Sir,

You leave the house.

I watch the house.

He came to the house. I watch.

He and she leave the house. I follow.

He and she get on train. I follow.

He and she go in hotel. I climb tree – look in window.

He kiss she, she kiss he. He strip she, she strip he.

He play with she, she play with he, I play with me.

I fall out of tree, not see, no fee.

SUBJECT: GARAGE DOOR

Noticing her boss's fly was open, the embarrassed secretary told him, "Your garage door is open."

The bewildered executive didn't know what she meant until she pointed down. He quickly zipped up and said, "I hope you didn't see my super deluxe Ferrari?"

"Nope." she replied. "Just an old pink Volkswagen with two flat tires."

SUBJECT: GOLF

A golfer hits a big slice on the first hole, and his ball ends up behind a small shed. He's about to chip out when the caddie says, "Wait! I'll open the window and the door, then you can hit a 3 wood right through the shed."

After the caddie opens the escape route, the golfer makes a big swing. The ball nearly makes it, but hits the windowsill, then bounces back and hits the golfer in the head.

The next thing the golfer knows, he's standing at the Pearly Gates. Saint Peter sees him with his 3 wood in hand and says, "I guess you think you're a pretty good golfer."

And the guy says, "Hey, I got here in two, didn't I?"

SUBJECT: APTLY CALLED 'GROANERS'... BUT WORTH A READ... AND MAYBE EVEN A LAUGH!!!

- Two antennas meet on a roof, fall in love and get married. The ceremony wasn't much, but the reception was excellent.

- Two hydrogen atoms walk into a bar. One says, "I've lost my electron." The other says, "Are you sure?" The first replies, "Yes, I'm positive..."

- A jumper cable walks into a bar. The bartender says, "I'll serve you, but don't start anything."

- Two peanuts walk into a bar, and one was a salted.

- A dyslexic man walks into a bra.

- A man walks into a bar with a slab of asphalt under his arm and says, "A beer please, and one for the road."

- Two cannibals are eating a clown. One says to the other, "Does this taste funny to you?"

- "Doc, I can't stop singing *The Green, Green Grass of Home*." "That sounds like Tom Jones Syndrome." "Is it common?" "*It's Not Unusual*."

- Two cows standing next to each other in a field, Daisy says to Dolly, "I was artificially inseminated this morning." "I don't believe you," said Dolly. "It's true, no bull!" exclaimed Daisy.

- An invisible man marries an invisible woman. The kids were nothing to look at either.

- Deja Moo: The feeling that you've heard this bull before.

- A man takes his Rottweiler to the vet and says, "My dog's cross-eyed, is there anything you can do for him?" "Well," says the vet, "let's have a look at him." So he picks the dog up and examines his eyes, then checks his teeth. Finally, he says, "I'm going to have to put him down." "What? Because he's cross-eyed?" "No, because he's really heavy."

- Apparently, one in five people in the world are Chinese. And there are five people in my family, so it must be one of them. It's either my Mum or my Dad, or maybe my older brother Colin or my younger brother Ho-Cha-Chu. But I'm pretty sure it's Colin.

- I went to buy some camouflage trousers the other day but I couldn't find any.

- I went to the butcher's the other day and I bet him 50 bucks that he couldn't reach the meat off the top shelf. He said, "No, the steaks are too high."

- A man woke up in a hospital after a serious accident. He shouted, "Doctor, doctor, I can't feel my legs!" The doctor replied, "I know you can't – I've cut off your arms!"

- I went to a seafood disco last week... and pulled a mussel.

- Two Eskimos sitting in a kayak were chilly, but when they lit a fire in the craft, it sank, proving that you can't have your kayak and heat it too.

- What do you call a fish with no eyes? A fish.

- A sandwich walks into a bar. The bartender says, "Sorry we don't serve food in here."

SUBJECT: MORE GOLF...

Upon returning the club house after the worst round of golf in his life, the golfer requested that the caddie give him the ball.

He then threw the ball into the lake. The golfer then asked the caddie for his clubs.

The caddie asked what he planned to do with the clubs, hes said, "throw them in the lake," which he did.

The golfer then started walking towards the lake, and the caddie asked, "what are you intending to do?"

"I'm going to drown myself" replied the golfer.

"You can't do that, you can't keep your head down long enough!"

SUBJECT: TAKING YOUR GOLF SERIOUSLY

Watching from the club house overlooking the tenth green, we saw a foursome approaching. Having marked their balls, suddenly one of the guys fell down and the three others started a fist fight.

The Golf Captain stormed out from the club house to separate the fighting men. "Why are you fighting?" he asked.

"You see," said one of them, "my partner just had a stroke and now these arseholes want to count it on the scorecard."

SUBJECT: THE GENIE

A woman rubbed a bottle and out popped a genie. The amazed woman asked if she got three wishes.

The genie said, "Nope, sorry, three-wish genies are a storybook myth. I'm a one-wish genie. So... what'll it be?"

The woman did not hesitate. She said, "I want peace in the Middle East. See this map? I want these countries to stop fighting with each other and I want all the Arabs to love the Jews and Americans and vice-versa. It will bring about world peace and harmony."

The genie looked at the map and exclaimed, "Lady, be reasonable. These countries have been at war for thousands of years. I'm out of shape after being in a bottle for five hundred years. I'm good but not THAT good! I don't think it can be done. Make another wish and please be reasonable."

The woman thought for a minute and said, "Well, I've never been able to find the right man. You know – one that's considerate and fun, likes to cook and help with the house cleaning, is great in bed, and gets along with my family, doesn't watch sports all the time, and is faithful. That is what I wish for... a good man."

The genie let out a sigh and said, "Let me see the fu*king map again."

SUBJECT: GOVERNMENTS AND HOW THEY WORK.

Once upon a time the government had a vast scrap yard in the middle of the bush. The officials said, "Someone may steal from it at night." So they created a night watchman position and hired the gentleman for the job.

Then the officials said, "How does the night watchman do his job without instruction." So they created a planning department and hired two people, one person to write the instructions, and one person to do time studies.

Then the officials said, "How are these people going to be paid?" So they created the following positions, a time keeper and a payroll officer, then hired two people.

Then the officials said, "Who will be accountable for all these people?" So they created an administrative section and hired three people, and Administrative Officer, Assistant Administrative Officer, and Legal Secretary.

Then the officials said, "We have had this command in operation for one year and we are $19,000 over budget, we must cutback overall cost." So they laid off the night watchman.

SUBJECT: GOVERNMENT POLICY

1. When you don't know what to do, walk fast and look worried.
2. The last person who quit, or was fired, will be held responsible for everything that goes wrong.
3. Gettng the job done is no excuse for not following the rules.
4. To err is human; to forgive is not our policy.

SUBJECT: GREEN SIDE

Dave the builder was going through a house he had just built with the woman who owned it with her husband. The lady of the house was telling him what colour to paint each room.

They went into the first room and she said, "I want this room to be painted a light blue."

The builder went to the front door and yelled, "GREEN SIDE UP!"

When he went to find her in the next room, she told him that it was to be magenta.

The builder went to the front door and yelled, "GREEN SIDE UP!"

When he went back down the hallway to find her, she told him that the next room was to be tan.

The builder went to the front door and yelled, "GREEN SIDE UP!"

When he came back, the lady was pretty curious, so she asked him "I keep telling you colours, but you go out the front and yell green side up, what's that for?

The builder said, "Oh, don't worry about that, I've got a couple of Kiwis laying the turf out front."

SUBJECT: GENERATION Y

(o)(o) = perfect breasts.

(@)(@) = big nipple breasts.

(q)(o) = pierced breasts.

($)($) - Elle McPherson's breasts.

(*)(*) = high nipple breasts.

(^)(^) = cold breasts.

\o/\o/ = grandma's breasts.

SUBJECT: GOTTA GET A BET ON!

A man is sitting reading his newspaper when his wife sneaks up behind him and whacks him on the head with a frying pan.

"What was that for?" he asks.

"That was for the piece of paper in your trouser pocket with the name Mary-Jane written on it," she replies.

"Don't be silly," he says, "Two weeks ago when I went to the races. Mary-Jane was the name of one of the horses I bet on."

His wife seemed satisfied at this and apologised.

Three days later he's again sitting in his chair reading when she nails him with an even bigger frying pan, knocking him out cold.

When he comes around he asks, "What was that for?"

"Your F*CKIN' horse phoned!"

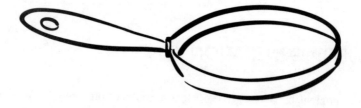

SUBJECT: THE HIPPIE AND THE NUN

A hippie hops onto a bus and sees a nun. He says to the nun, "Will you have sex with me?" The nun immediately declines and hops off at the next stop.

The hippy tries to follow her but is stopped by the bus driver (male). He says to the hippy, "I know how you can get her to have sex with you!!!" The hippy anxiously listens. "Every Tuesday the nun goes to the cemetery to prey. All you have to do is go there and pretend to be God and demand her to have sex with you."

The hippy thinks this is a great idea and does so. He went to the cemetery dressed in robes and waited for the nun. He saw her coming up the path so he hid behind a tree and listened. When she was in the middle of her prayer he jumped out from behind the tree and said, "I am God. I demand you to have sex with me."

The nun hesitated but agreed only on the condition that they have anal sex because she did not want to lose her virginity.

The hippy agreed and they got on with things. When they had finished the hippy jumped off and screamed, "HA HA... I'M THE HIPPY" and the nun jumped up and said, "HA HA... I'M THE BUS DRIVER."

SUBJECT: HUNTING

Two hunters are out in the woods when one of them collapses. He doesn't seem to be breathing and his eyes are glazed.

The other guy whips out his phone and calls the emergency services. He gasps, "My friend is dead! What can I do?"

The operator says, "Calm down, I can help. First, let's make sure he's dead."

There is a silence, then a shot is heard. Back on the phone, the guy says, "OK, now what?"

SUBJECT: HUSBAND AND WIFE

Dear Ex-Husband,

I'm writing you this letter to tell you that I'm leaving you for good. I've been a good woman to you for seven years and I have nothing to show for it. These last two weeks have been hell.

Your boss called to tell me that you had quit your job today and that was the last straw. Last week, you came home and didn't notice that I had gotten my hair and nails done, cooked your favourite meal and even wore a brand new negligee. You came home and ate in two minutes, and went straight to sleep after watching the game. You don't tell me you love me any more, you don't touch me or anything. You're cheating or you don't love me any more, whatever the case is, I'm gone.

P. S. If you're trying to find me, don't. Your BROTHER and I are moving away to West Virginia together! Have a great life!

Your EX-Wife

Dear Ex-Wife,

Nothing has made my day more than receiving your letter.

It's true that you and I have been married for seven years, although a good woman is a far cry from what you've been. I watch sports so much to try to drown out your constant nagging. Too bad that doesn't work. I did notice when you cut off all of your hair last week, the first thing that came to mind was, "You look just like a man!" My mother raised me not to say anything if you can't say anything nice.

When you cooked my favourite meal, you must have gotten me confused with MY BROTHER, because I stopped eating pork seven years ago. I went to sleep on you when you had on that new negligee because the price tag was still on it. I prayed that it was a coincidence that my brother had just borrowed fifty dollars from me that morning and your negligee was $49.99.

After all of this, I still loved you and felt that we could work it out. So when I discovered that I had hit the lotto for ten million dollars, I quit my job and bought us two tickets to Jamaica. But when I got home you were gone. Everything happens for a reason I guess.

I hope you have the filling life you always wanted. My lawyer said with your letter that you wrote, you won't get a dime from me. So take care.

P. S. I don't know if I ever told you this but Carl, my brother was born Carla. I hope that's not a problem.

SUBJECT: HORSE SENSE

The aspiring psychiatrists from various colleges were in their class on emotional extremes.

"Just to establish the parameters", said the professor, "what is the opposite of joy?"

"Sadness," said the student from Melbourne.

"And the opposite of depression?" he asked the young lady from Sydney.

"Elation," she said.

"And you sir," he looked at the young man from the Snowy Mountains Agriculture College, "what is the opposite of woe?"

"That would be giddy-up," he replied.

SUBJECT: HEADLINES TO GRAB YOUR ATTENTION

New Sign Proposed For Suburban Speed Zones: Buggered If We Know Either

McDonalds Customer Asks For Upsize Salad. Employee Faints

iPod Owner Dies Before Hearing Full Play List

Hollywood Scandal: Celebrity Confesses – I Haven't Had Sex With Paris Hilton

Man Falls Into XXX Large Latte And drowns

New Hair Colour Discovered: Your Own

Buy Full Tank Of Petrol. Get Car Free

Crocodile Mauls Steve Irwin. Actually Improves His Haircut

After $10 million Research New Toothbrush Looks Identical To Old Toothbrush

Disney Prequels For 2005: Bambi's Mother Is Alive, Pinocchio Just A Bit Of Wood and Nemo's Still Here

Latin Dancing Gene Discovered With Fake Tan Wrapped Around Other Genes

Ten Commandments Revised To Ten Lifestyle Options

New Personal Digital Assistant Camera Phone Shock: So Complicated No One Can Turn It On

Spider Man's Affair With Catwoman Produces Web-Firing Super hero Who Won't Get Out Of Your Chair

Green Shopping Bags Prove More Environmentally Friendly Than Non-Green Shopping Bags

Rod Stewart Marries Short, Flat Chested Brunette: Blames New Glasses

Celebrity Chef Subdued With Capsicum Spray. Garnished With Coriander

Brazilian Girls On Waxing: Actually, We Prefer The Tasmanian

Medical Breakthrough: Doctor On Time For Patient's Appointment

New Anti–Wrinkle Cream So Effective Women Shrink Three Sizes

Obese Find A Way To Improve Health Statistics: Just Eat More Statisticians

SUBJECT: TRUTH IN HUMOUR

1. Now that food has replaced sex in my life, I can't even get into my own pants.

2. Marriage changes passion. Suddenly you're in bed with a relative.

3. I saw a woman wearing a sweat shirt with 'Guess' on it. So I said, "Implants?" She hit me.

4. I don't do drugs. I get the same effect just standing up fast.

5. Sign in a Chinese pet store, "Buy one dog, get one flea..."

6. I live in my own little world. But it's OK. They know me here.

7. I got a sweater for Christmas. I really wanted a screamer or a moaner.

8. If flying is so safe, why do they call the airport the terminal?

9. I don't approve of political jokes. I've seen too many of them get elected.

10. There are two sides to every divorce: Yours and Shit Head's.

11. I love being married. It's so great to find that one special person you want to annoy for the rest of your life.

12. I am a nobody, and nobody is perfect; therefore, I am perfect.

13. Everyday I beat my own previous record for number of consecutive days I have stayed alive.

14. How come we choose from just two people to run for president and 50 for Miss America?

15. Isn't having a smoking section in a restaurant like having a peeing section in a swimming pool?

16. Why is it that most nudists are people you don't want to see naked?

17. Snowmen fall from Heaven unassembled.

18. Every time I walk into a singles bar I can hear Mum's wise words: Don't pick that up, you don't know where it's been!"

19. A good friend will come and bail you out of jail... but, a true friend will be sitting next to you saying, "Damn... that was fun!"

20. When I was young we used to go 'skinny dipping', now I just 'chunky dunk'.

21. Don't argue with an idiot; people watching may not be able to tell the difference.

22. Wouldn't it be nice if whenever we messed up our life we could simply press 'Ctrl Alt Delete' and start all over?

23. Stress is when you wake up screaming and then you realize you haven't fallen asleep yet.

24. Just remember... if the world didn't suck, we'd all fall off.

SUBJECT: NO SENSE OF HUMOUR...

My wife and I are watching, *Who Wants To Be A Millionaire* while we are in bed. I turned to her and said, "Do you want to have sex?"

"No." She answered.

I then said, "Is that your final answer?"

"Yes," She replied.

Then I said, "I'd like to phone a friend."

That's the last thing I remember.

SUBJECT: HILARIOUS

A blind man enters a lesbian bar by mistake. And finds his way to the bar stool, and orders a drink. After sitting there for a while, he yells to the bartender in a loud voice, "Hey bartender, you wanna here a dumb blonde joke?!!

The bar immediately falls deathly quiet. In a very deep, husky voice the women next to him says, "Before you tell that joke, sir, I think it is fair, given you are blind, you should know five things....

1. The bartender is a blonde woman.
2. The bouncer is a blonde woman.
3. The woman sitting next to me is blonde, and is a professional weightlifter.
4. The lady on your right is a blonde, and is a professional wrestler and
5. I'm six foot, 200 pounds, blonde woman with a PhD, a black belt in karate and very bad attitude! Now think about it seriously Mr. do you still want to tell that joke?" The blind man thinks for a second, shakes his head, and says, "Naaaah... not if I'm gunna have to explain it five times."

SUBJECT: THE HUSBAND

The wife comes home early and finds her husband in their master bedroom making love to a beautiful, young woman!

You unfaithful, disrespectful pig! What are you doing? How dare you do this to me the faithful wife, the mother of your children! I'm leaving this house, I want a divorce!"

The husband, replies, "Wait, wait a minute! Before you leave, at least listen to what happened"

"Hummmmm, I don't know, well it'll be the last thing I will hear from you. But make it fast, you unfaithful pig you"

The husband begins to tell his story . . . "While driving home this young lady asks for a ride. I saw her so defenceless that I went ahead and allowed her in my car. I noticed that she was very thin, not well dressed and very dirty. She mentioned that she had not eaten for three days with great compassion and hurt, I brought her home and warmed up the enchiladas that I made for you last night that you wouldn't eat because you're afraid you'll gain weight. The poor thing, practically devours them. Since she was very dirty I asked her to take a shower.

While she was showering, I noticed her clothes were dirty and full of holes so I threw her clothes away. Since she needed clothes, I gave her the pair of jeans that you have had for a few years, that you can no longer wear because they are too tight on you, I also gave her the blouse that I gave you on our anniversary and you don't wear because I don't have good taste. I gave her the pullover that my sister gave you for Christmas that you will not wear just to bother my sister and I also gave her the boots that you bought at the expensive boutique that you never wore again after you saw your co-worker wearing the same pair."

The husband continues his story . . . . .
"The young woman was very grateful to me and I walked her to the door. When we got to the door she turned around and with tears coming out of her eyes, she asks me:

"Sir, do you have anything else that your wife does not use?"

SUBJECT: HELLO... A STUPID QUESTION, AND GET AN APPROPRIATE ANSWER

I was in Woolworths buying a large bag of Lucky Dog for my Labrador Retriever and was in line to check out. A woman behind me asked if I had a dog.

On impulse, I told her that no, I was starting The Lucky Dog Diet again, although I probably shouldn't because I'd ended up in the hospital last time, but that I'd lost 20 kilos before I awakened in an intensive care ward with tubes coming out of most of my orifices and IVs in both arms.

I told her that it was essentially a perfect diet and that the way that it works is to load your pants pockets with Lucky Dog nuggets and simply eat one or two every time you feel hungry and that the food is nutritionally complete so I was going to try it again. I have to mention here that practically everyone in the line was by now enthralled with my story.

Horrified, she asked if I'd been poisoned and was that why I was in the hospital.

I said no... I'd been sitting in the street licking my balls and a car hit me.

SUBJECT: HOW TRUE IS THIS?

Simplified Tax Form.

Question: How much money did you make?

$_____

Action: Send it to us.

SUBJECT: HELLO THIS IS DADDY!!

Pick up

"Hello"

"Hi honey, this is Daddy, is Mummy near the phone?"

"No daddy, She's upstairs in the bedroom with uncle Paul."

After a brief pause, Daddy says, "but honey, you haven't got an Uncle Paul."

"Oh yes I do, and he's upstairs in the room with Mummy, right now."

Brief Pause

"Oh okay then, this is what I want you to do. Put the phone down on the table, run upstairs and knock on the bedroom door, and shout to Mummy that Daddy's car just pulled into the driveway."

"Okay daddy, just a minute."

A few minutes later the little girl comes back to the phone.

"I did it daddy."

"And what happened honey?" he asked.

"Well Mummy got all scared, jumped out of bed with no clothes on and ran around screaming. Then she tripped on the rug, hit her head on the dresser and now she isn't moving at all!"

"Oh my god!!! What about uncle Paul?"

"He jumped out of the bed with no clothes on too. He was scared and he jumped out of the back window and into the swimming pool. But I guess he didn't know that you took out the water last week to clean it, he hit the bottom of the pool and I think he's dead."

****Long Pause***** Longer Pause*******

Then Daddy says, "Swimming Pool?... Is this 486 5731?"

SUBJECT: HISTORY OF THE MIDDLE FINGER

Well, now... here's something I never knew before, and now that I know it, I feel compelled to send it on to my more intelligent friends in the hope that they, too, will feel edified.

Isn't history more fun when you know something about it?

Giving the finger before the Battle of Agincourt in 1415, the French, anticipating victory over the English, proposed to cut off the middle finger of all captured English soldiers. Without the middle finger it would be impossible to draw the renowned English longbow and therefore they would be incapable of fighting in the future.

This famous weapon was made of the native English Yew tree, and the act of drawing the longbow was known as 'plucking the yew" (or 'pluck yew').

Much to the bewilderment of the French, the English won a major upset and began mocking the French by waving their middle fingers at the defeated French, saying, "See, we can still pluck yew!"

"PLUCK YEW!"

Since 'pluck yew' is rather difficult to say, the difficult consonant cluster at the beginning has gradually hanged to a labio-dental fricative 'f*ck', and thus the words often used in conjunction with the one-finger-salute!

It is also because of the pheasant feathers on the arrows used with the longbow that the symbolic gesture is known as 'giving the bird'.

SO REMEMBER TO SALUTE ALL THE PHEASANT PLUCKERS YOU KNOW !

And yew thought yew knew everything!

SUBJECT: THE IRISHMAN

Mick walks into a bar in Dublin, orders three pints of Guinness and sits in the back of the room, drinking a sip out of each one in turn.

When he finishes them, he comes back to the bar and orders three more. The bartender asks him, "You know a pint goes flat after the draw. It would taste better if you bought one at a time."

Mick replies, "Well, you see, I have two brothers. One is in America, the other in Australia, and I'm here in Dublin."

"When we all left home, we promised that we'd drink this way to remember the days when we drank together." The bartender admits this is a nice custom, and leaves it there.

Mick becomes a regular at the bar, and always drinks the same way: ordering three pints and drinking them in turn. One day, he comes in and orders two pints. All the others notice and fall silent.

When Mick comes back to the bar for the second round, the bartender says, "I don't want to intrude in your grief, but I wanted to offer my condolences on your great loss." Mick looks confused for a moment, then light dawns in the eye, and he laughs.

"Oh, no," he says, "Everyone's fine. I've just quit drinking."

SUBJECT: MALE INTERPRETATIONS

LOVE – When you're only interested in doing things with your partner.

LUST – When you're only interested in doing things TO your partner.

MARRIAGE – When you're only interested in your golf score.

SUBJECT: IS THAT JESUS

An Australian, an Irishman and an Englishman were sitting in a bar. There was only one other person in the bar; a man. The three men kept looking at this other man, for he seemed terribly familiar. They stared and stared, wondering where they had seen him before, when suddenly the Irishman cried out, "My God, I know who that man is. It's Jesus!" The others looked again and, sure enough, it was Jesus himself, sitting alone at a table.

The Irishman call out, "Hey! You!!! Are you Jesus?" The man looks over at him, smiles a small smile and nods his head. "Yes, I am Jesus" he says.

The Irishman calls the bartender over and says to him, "I'd like you to give Jesus over there a pint of Guinness from me." So the bartender pours Jesus a Guinness and takes it over to his table. Jesus looks over, raises his glass, smiles thank you and drinks.

The Englishman then calls out, "Errr, excuse me Sir, but would you be Jesus?" Jesus smiles and says, "Yes, I am Jesus." The Englishman beckons the bartender and tells him to send over a pint of Newcastle Brown Ale for Jesus, which the bartender duly does. As before, Jesus accepts the drink and smiles over at the men.

Then the Australian calls out, "Oi, you! D'ya reckon you're Jesus, or what?" Jesus nods and says, "Yes, I am Jesus." The Australian is mighty impressed and has the bartender send over a pot of Victoria Bitter for Jesus, which he accepts with pleasure.

Some time later, after finishing the drinks, Jesus leaves his seat and approaches the three men. He reaches for the hand of the Irishman and shakes it, thanking him for the Guinness. When he lets go, the Irishman gives a cry of amazement. "Oh God, the arthritis is gone," he says. "The arthritis I've had for years is gone. It's a miracle!"

Jesus then shakes the hand of the Englishman, thanking him for the Newcastle Brown Ale. Upon letting go, the Englishman's eyes widen in shock. "By jove!" he exclaims, "The migraine I've had for over 40 years is completely gone. It's a Miracle!"

Jesus then approaches the Australian, who has a terrified look on his face. The Aussie whispers, "F*ck off, mate. I'm on workers comp."

SUBJECT: DEAR JOHN

This is fabulous ...

A Marine stationed in Afghanistan recently received a 'Dear John' letter from his girlfriend back home. It read as follows:

Dear Ricky,

I can no longer continue our relationship. The distance between us is just too great. I must admit that I have cheated on you twice, since you've been gone, and it's not fair to either of us. I'm sorry.

Please return the picture of me that I sent to you.

Love,
Becky

The Marine, with hurt feelings, asked his fellow Marines for any snapshots they could spare of their girlfriends, sisters, ex-girlfriends, aunts, cousins etc. In addition to the picture of Becky, Ricky included all the other pictures of the pretty gals he had collected from his buddies.

There were 57 photos in that envelope... along with this note:

Dear Becky,

I'm so sorry, but I can't quite remember who the f*ck you are. Please take your picture from the pile, and send the rest back to me.

Take Care,
Ricky

Touché

SUBJECT: A LITTLE JOKE

A man is lying in bed in the hospital with an oxygen mask over his mouth.

A young nurse appears to sponge his hands and feet.

"Nurse," he mumbles from behind the mask, "Are my testicles black?"

Embarrassed, the young nurse replies, "I don't know, I'm only here to wash your hands and feet."

He struggles again to ask, "Nurse, Are my testicles black?"

Finally, she pulls back the covers, raises his gown, holds his penis in one hand and his testicles in her other hand and takes a close look, and say's, "There's nothing wrong with them!"

Finally, the man pulls off his oxygen mask and replies, "That was very nice but, are my... test... results... back?"

SUBJECT: ANOTHER LITTLE JOKE

A man walks up to a woman in his office and tells her that her hair really smells nice.

The woman immediately goes to the boss to file a sexual harassment case.

The supervisor puzzled by this, asks, "What's wrong with a co-worker telling you that your hair smells nice?"

She replied, "He's a midget."

SUBJECT: JOHNNY

Little Johnny's neighbour had a baby. Unfortunately, the baby was born without ears. When mother and new baby came home from the hospital, Johnny's family where invited over to see the baby.

Before they left their house, Little Johnny's dad had a talk with him and explained that the baby had no ears. His dad also told him that if he so much as mentioned anything about the baby's missing ears or even said the word ears, he would get the smacking of his life when they came back home. Little Johnny told his dad he understood completely.

When Johnny looked in the crib he said, "What a beautiful baby." The mother said, "Why, thank you, Little Johnny." Johnny said, "He has beautiful little feet and beautiful little hands, a cute little nose and really beautiful eyes. Can he see?"

"Yes," the mother replied, "we are so thankful – the Doctor said he will have 20/20 vision." "That's great," said Little Johnny, "cos he'd be f*cked if he needed glasses..."

SUBJECT: JOHN

John was in a bar looking very dejected.

His friend, Steve, walked over and asked, "What's wrong?"

"It's my mother-in-law," John replied, while shaking his head sadly.

"I have a real problem with her."

"Cheer up," Steve said. "Everyone has problems with their mother-in-law."

"Maybe," John answered. "But I got mine pregnant."

SUBJECT: QUICK JOKES

How many men does it take to open a beer?
None. It should be opened when she brings it.

How do you fix a woman's watch?
You don't. There is a clock on the oven.

What has five legs?
A happy bull terrier

Scientists have discovered a food that diminishes a woman's sex
drive by 90 per cent.
It's called a Wedding Cake.

Why do men die before their wives?
They want to.

Women will never be equal to men until they can walk down the
street with a bald head and a beer gut, and still think they are sexy.

What is the difference between blokes and women.
A woman wants one bloke to satisfy his every need. A bloke wants
every woman to satisfy his one need.

SUBJECT: JIMMY

A rich man living in Darwin decided that he wanted to throw a party and invited all of his buddies and neighbours. He held the party around the pool in the back yard of his mansion.

Everyone was having a good time drinking, dancing, eating prawns, oysters and BBQ and flirting. At the height of the party, the host said, "I have a 15 ft. man-eating crocodile in my pool and I'll give a million dollars to anyone who has the balls to jump in."

The words were barely out of his mouth when there was a loud splash and he turned around and saw his mate Jimmy in the pool! Jimmy was fighting the croc and kicking its arse! Jimmy was jabbing the croc in the eyes with his thumbs, throwing punches, doing all kinds of shit, like head butts and choke holds, biting the croc on the tail and flipping the croc through the air like some kind of Judo Instructor.

The water was churning and splashing everywhere. Both Jimmy }and the croc were screaming and raising hell. Finally Jimmy strangled the croc and let it float to the top like a K-mart goldfish. Jimmy then slowly climbed out of the pool. Everybody was just staring at him in disbelief.

Finally the host says, "Well, Jimmy, I reckon I owe you a million dollars." "Nah, you all right, I don't want it," said Jimmy. The rich man said, "Man, I have to give you something. You won the bet. How about half a million bucks then?" "No thanks. I don't want it," answered Jimmy.

The host said, "Come on, I insist on giving you something. That was amazing. How about a new Porsche, a Rolex and some stock options?"

Again Jimmy said no.

Confused, the rich man asked, "Well Jimmy, then what do you want?" Jimmy said, "I want the name of the %*#$ who pushed me in the pool."

SUBJECT: MORE JOKES

How do you know when a woman is about to say something smart?
When she starts a sentence with, "A man once told me..."

Why is a laundromat a really bad place to pick up a woman?
Because a woman who can't even afford a washing machine will probably never be able to support you.

Why do men fart more than women?
Because women can't shut up long enough to build up the required pressure.

What's worse than a male chauvinist pig?
A woman who won't do what she's told.

If your dog is barking at the back door and your wife is yelling at the front door, who do you let in first?
The dog, of course. He'll shut up once you let him in.

I married a Miss Right.
I just didn't know her first name was Always.

SUBJECT: FATHER JOHN...

It was time for Father John's Saturday night bath and young Sister Magdalene had prepared the bath water and towels just the way an old nun had instructed. Sister Magdalene was also instructed not to look at Father John's nakedness if she could help it, do whatever he told her to do and pray.

The next morning the old nun asked Sister Magdalene how the Saturday night bath had gone.

"Oh, Sister" said the young nun dreamily. "I've been saved."

"Saved? And how did that come about?" asked the old nun.

"Well, when Father John was soaking in the tub, he asked me to wash him, and while I was washing him he guided my hand down between his legs where he said the Lord keeps the Key to Heaven."

"Did he now..." said the old nun evenly.

Sister Magdalene continued, "And Father John said that if the Key to Heaven fit my lock, the portals of Heaven would be opened to me and I would be assured of salvation and eternal peace. And then Father John guided his key to Heaven into my lock."

"Is that a fact..." said the old nun, even more evenly.

"At first it hurt terribly, but Father John said the pathway to salvation was often painful but that the glory of God would soon swell my heart with ecstasy. And it did, it felt good being saved."

"That son-of-a..." muttered the old nun, "he told ME it was Gabriel's Horn and I've been blowing it for forty years!"

SUBJECT: JOKE

The parish priest went on a fishing trip. On the last day of his trip he hooked a monster fish and proceeded to reel it in. The guide, holding a net, yelled, "Look at the size of that son of a bitch!"

"Son, I'm a priest. Your language is uncalled for!"

Thinking quickly, the guide replied, "No, Father, that's what kind of fish it is – a Son of a Bitch fish!"

"Really? Well then, help me land this Son of a Bitch!"

Once in the boat, they marvelled at the size of the monster.

"Father, that's the biggest Son of a Bitch I've ever seen."

"Yes, it is a big Son of a Bitch. What should I do with it?"

"Why, eat it of course. You've never tasted anything as good as Son of a Bitch!"

Elated, the priest headed home to the rectory. While unloading his gear and his prize catch, Sister Mary inquired about his trip.

"Take a look at this big Son of a Bitch I caught!" Sister Mary gasped and clutched her rosary, "Father!"

"It's OK, Sister. That's what kind of fish it is – a Son of a Bitch fish!"

"Oh, well then, what are you going to do with that big Son of a Bitch?"

"Why, eat it of course. The guide said nothing compares to the taste of a Son of a Bitch."

Sister Mary informed the priest that the new Bishop was scheduled to visit in a few days, and that they should fix the Son of a Bitch for his dinner. "I'll even clean the Son of a Bitch," she said. As she was cleaning the huge fish, the Friar walked in. "What are you doing Sister?" "Father wants me to clean this big Son of a Bitch for the new Bishop's dinner.

SUBJECT: IT'S ONLY A SHORT RIDE TO THE DARK SIDE

Little Johnny, "Grandpa, can I try one of your cigarettes?"

"Can you touch your arsehole with your penis?" the grandfather asks.

"No" says Little Johnny. "Then you're not big enough." says the grandfather.

A few minutes pass, and the man takes a beer out of his cooler and opens it.

Little Johnny says, "Grandpa, can I have some of your beer?"

"Can you touch your arsehole with your penis?" he asks.

"No" says Little Johnny. "Then you're not old enough."

Time passes and they continue to fish. Little Johnny gets hungry and he reaches into his lunch box, takes out a bag of cookies and eats one.

The grandfather looks at him and says, "They look good, can I have one of your cookies?"

"Can you touch your arsehole with your penis?" asks Johnny.

"I most certainly can!" says the grandfather proudly.

"Then go f*ck yourself," says Johnny, "these are my cookies!"

SUBJECT: ANOTHER MAN WALKS INTO A BAR JOKE

A man walks into a bar, with a little dog on a leash.

He says to the barman, "would you like to buy my dog, he's ten dollars, he can talk!"

The barman's obviously heard stuff like this before, and says, "Yeah yeah, ten dollars, talking dog, rack off, I'm busy."

At this point the dog pipes up and says very politely, "Please, sir, please buy me. He beats me. He leaves me out in the cold, and he doesn't feed me!"

The barman is astonished and says, "You could make a million dollars with a talking dog, why are you selling him for ten dollars?"

The man replies, "Cos I'm sick to death of all the bloody lies he tells!"

SUBJECT: AUSTRALIAN JOKE

Three blokes were working on yet another high rise building project in Sydney – Steve, Bill and Charlie.

Steve falls off and is killed instantly.

As the ambulance takes Steve's body away, Charlie says, "Someone should go and tell his wife."

Bill says, "OK, I'm pretty good at that sensitive stuff, I'll do it."

Two hours later, he comes back carrying a carton of beer.

Charlie says, "Where did you get that, Bill?"

"Steve's wife gave it to me."

"That's unbelievable, you told the lady her husband was dead and she gave you the beer?"

Bill says, "Well not exactly. When she answered the door, I said to her, 'You must be Steve's widow.'"

She said, "No, I'm not a widow."

And I said, "Wanna bet me a carton of beer?"

SUBJECT: THE JOCKEY

A jockey riding the favourite in the Cheltenham steeplechase was well ahead of the field. Suddenly, he was hit on the head by a chicken, and a hail of cherry tomatoes!

He managed to stay in control of his horse, and once again regained the lead. All of a sudden, coming over the last fence, he was hit on the head by a box of paper serviettes, and a dozen fruit mince pies!

Once again, his skill showed through, and he managed to keep control, and again moved into the lead. He was running through the last corner, holding his lead, when he was struck on the head by a bottle of Asti Spumante and a chocolate cheesecake!

With only metres to go to finish the race, the distraction was too much for him, and he succeeded in coming only second.

He immediately went to the Stewards to complain that he had been seriously hampered.

SUBJECT: LITTLE JOHNNY

Little Johnny has just been toilet trained and decides to use the big toilet like his Daddy. He pushes up the seat and balances his little penis on the rim.

Just then the toilet seat slams down, and little Johnny lets out a scream.

His mother comes running to find Johnny hopping round the room clutching his genitals and howling.

He looks up at her with his little tear stained face and sniffles, "K-k-k-k-kiss {sniff} it better."

Little Johnny's mother shouts, "Don't start your father's shit with me!"

SUBJECT: JUSTICE?

How to impress a woman:

Compliment her, respect her, honour her, caress her, kiss her, love her, tease her, comfort her, protect her, hug her, hold her, spend money on her, listen to her, stand by her, go to the ends of the earth for her.

How to impress a man:

Turn up naked with a carton of beer.

SUBJECT: JIBES

In the beginning, God created the earth and rested.
Then God created Man and rested.
Then God created Woman.
Since then, neither God nor Man has rested.

Nothing is more wasted than a smile on a girl with a forty inch bust.

My doctor cancelled me as a patient. He said I'd gone too long without having anything expensive.

A little boy asked his father, "Daddy, how much does it cost to get married?"

Father replied, "I don't know son, I'm still paying."

A young son asked, "Is it true Dad, that in some parts of Africa a man doesn't know his wife until he marries her?"

Dad replied, "That happens in every country, son."

Then there was a woman who said, "I never knew what real happiness was until I got married, and by then, it was too late."

First guy says, "My wife's an angel!"
Second guy remarks, "You're lucky, mine's still alive."

SUBJECT: DOUBLE JEOPARDY

At a rape trial the young victim was asked by the public prosecutor what the defendant said before the alleged assault. Too embarrassed to answer aloud, the victim asked if she could write out the answer. After reading the note, the judge instructed the jury foreman to read it and pass it among the rest of the jurors.

One juror, who had dozed off, was nudged by the woman juror sitting next to him. He took the note from her and read, "I'm going to f*ck you like you've never been f*cked before."

The juror smiled at the woman and slipped the note in his pocket.

"Will juror number 12 please pass the note to me!" ordered the judge.

"I can't, Your Honour," the juror answered. "It's personal."

SUBJECT: JOKE

Q. Why is the part between the bottom of a woman's boobs and the top of her vagina called a waist?

A. Because you could easily fit another set of tits there!

Q. What's the difference between panties and a stage curtain.?

A. When you pull down the stage curtain, the show is over... but when you pull down the panties it is SHOW TIME!

When God created women,
he crossed a dung beetle with a cow
and got this cute little thing with tits,
that runs around looking for shit all day.

SUBJECT: KATRINA – THEY'VE STARTED...

Bush has just released a statement following his investigation into the New Orleans disaster – the blame is being put on a Muslim suicide plumber.

President Bush has asked for pop groups to stage a benefit concert for the victims of New Orleans however Katrina and the Waves have been told to f*ck off.

Mayor of New Orleans has denied rumours the Mardi Gras is cancelled. He expects a record number of floats this year on Main St.

Five black men in purple dinner jackets and bow ties were found floating today under a pier in New Orleans, DNA tests later identified them as The drifters.

Rumour has it they where under the board walk down by the sea.

Eric Burden and the animals are re-releasing their earlier hit, it begins, "There was a house in New Orleans."

Hurricane Katrina, typical female!

When she came she was warm wild and wet.
When she left she took the house and contents with her.

Two plane loads of volunteers left Liverpool airport today bound for New Orleans to assist with the looting.

SUBJECT: KING ARTHUR AND THE WITCH:

Young King Arthur was ambushed and imprisoned by the monarch of a neighbouring kingdom. The monarch could have killed him but was moved by Arthur's youth and ideals. So, the monarch offered him his freedom, as long as he could answer a very difficult question. Arthur would have a year to figure out the answer and, if after a year, he still had no answer, he would be put to death.

The question? What do women really want? Such a question would perplex even the most knowledgeable man, and to young Arthur, it seemed an impossible query. But, since it was better than death, he accepted the monarch's proposition to have an answer by year's end.

He returned to his kingdom and began to poll everyone: the princess, the priests, the wise men and even the court jester. He spoke with everyone, but no one could give him a satisfactory answer.

Many people advised him to consult the old witch, for only she would have the answer. But the price would be high, as the witch was famous throughout the kingdom for the exorbitant prices she charged. The last day of the year arrived and Arthur had no choice but to talk to the witch. She agreed to answer the question, but he would have to agree to her price first.

The old witch wanted to marry Sir Lancelot, the most noble of the Knights of the Round Table and Arthur's closest friend! Young Arthur was horrified. She was hunchbacked and hideous, had only one tooth, smelled like sewage, made obscene noises, etc. He had never encountered such a repugnant creature in all his life.

He refused to force his friend to marry her and endure such a terrible burden, but Lancelot, learning of the proposal, spoke with Arthur. He said nothing was too big of a sacrifice compared to Arthur's life and the preservation of the Round Table.

Hence, a wedding was proclaimed and the witch answered Arthur's question thus:

"What a woman really wants", she answered... "is to be in charge of her own life."

Everyone in the kingdom instantly knew that the witch had uttered a great truth and that Arthur's life would be spared.
And so it was, the neighbouring monarch granted Arthur his freedom and Lancelot and the witch had a wonderful wedding.

The honeymoon hour approached and Lancelot, steeling himself for a horrific experience, entered the bedroom. But, what a sight awaited him. The most beautiful woman he had ever seen lay before him on the bed. The astounded Lancelot asked what had happened.

The beauty replied that since he had been so kind to her when she appeared as a witch, she would henceforth, be her horrible deformed self only half the time and the beautiful maiden the other half.

Which would he prefer? Beautiful during the day... or night?

Lancelot pondered the predicament. During the day, a beautiful woman to show off to his friends, but at night, in the privacy of his castle, an old witch? Or, would he prefer having a hideous witch during the day, but by night, a beautiful woman for him to enjoy wondrous intimate moments?

What would YOU do?

What Lancelot chose is below. BUT... make YOUR choice before you scroll down below. OKAY?

Noble Lancelot said that he would allow HER to make the choice herself.

Upon hearing this, she announced that she would be beautiful all the time because he had respected her enough to let her be in charge of her own life.

Now... what is the moral to this story?

Scroll down

The moral is...
If you don't let a woman have her own way...
Things are going to get ugly.

SUBJECT: MAKE ME A KING

At his meeting with Queen Elizabeth recently, John Howard turned to the Queen and said, "As I'm the Prime Minister, I'm thinking of changing how my great country is referred to, and I'm thinking that it should be a Kingdom."

The Queen replied, "I'm sorry Mr. Howard, but to be a Kingdom, you have to have a King in charge – and you're not a King."

John Howard thought a while and then said, "How about a Principality then?"

To which the Queen replied, "Again, to be a Principality you have to be a Prince – and you're not a Prince, Mr. Howard."

Howard thought long and hard and came up with, "How about an Empire then?"

The Queen, getting a little annoyed by now, replied, "Sorry again, Mr. Howard, but to be an Empire you must have an Emperor in charge and you are not an Emperor."

Before Howard could utter another word, The Queen said, "I think you're doing quite nicely as a Country."

SUBJECT: KLOPMAN DIAMOND

A business man boarded a jet to fly to America. Next to him on the plane was a gorgeous woman wearing the most stunning, large diamond ring he had ever seen. He asked her about it.

"It's the Klopman Diamond," she said, "and it comes with a curse."

"What's the curse?" he asked.

"Mr Klopman" she replied.

SUBJECT: KNOWING YOUR MEDICATION

In pharmacology, all drugs have two names, a trade name and a generic name.

For example the trade name is Tylenol and the generic name is acetaminophen. Aleve is also called naproxen. Amoxil is amoxicillin and Advil is ibuprofen.

The FDA has been looking for a generic name for the Viagra drug, which the men use widely nowadays. After careful consideration the team of experts have settled on the generic name of mycoxafloppin. Also considered were, mycoxafailin, mydixadrupin, mydixarizin and dixafix and of course the most wanted ibepokin.

Pfizer Corp. announced today that V will be soon available in liquid form and will be marketed by Pepsi as a power beverage suitable for use as a mixer. It will now be possible for a man to literally pour himself a 'stiff one'.

Obviously, we can no longer call this a soft drink and it gives a new meaning to the names of cocktails, highballs and the good old fashioned stiff drink. Pepsi will market the new concoction by the name of: Mount and Do.

SUBJECT: KEEPING ON

Q: How does a man keep his youth?
A: By giving her furs and diamonds.

Q: Why do men keep whistling on the toilet?
A: It keeps reminding them which end to wipe.

SUBJECT: THE LAWYER

A lawyer dies and goes to Heaven. "There must be some mistake," the lawyer argues. "I'm too young to die. I'm only fifty five."

"Fifty five?" says Saint Peter. "No, according to our calculations, you're eighty two."

"How'd you get that?" the lawyer asks.

Answers St. Peter, "We added up your billable hours."

SUBJECT: FACTS OF LIFE

Little Simon came running into the house and asked his Mummy, "Can little girls have babies?"

"Of course not," his mother replied.

Simon ran outside and his mum heard him yell to his friends, "It's okay, we can play that game again."

SUBJECT: LITTLE JOHNNY

Little John raised his hand in the class room and yelled out, "Miss, I need a piss."

She replied, "Johnny, the correct word is urinate. Use it in a sentence and you may leave the class."

He said, "You're an eight, but if you had bigger boobs you'd be a ten."

SUBJECT: THE LOBSTER AND THE CRAB

Declan the humble crab and Kate the Lobster Princess were madly, deeply and passionately in Love. For months they enjoyed an idyllic relationship until one day Kate scuttled over to Declan in tears.

"We can't see each other any more..." she sobbed.

"Why?" gasped Declan.

"Daddy says that crabs are too common," she wailed. "He claims you, are a mere crab, and a poor one at that, and crabs are the lowest class of crustacean... and that no daughter of his will marry someone who can only walk sideways."

Declan was shattered, and scuttled sideways away into the darkness and to drink himself into a filthy state of aquatic oblivion.

That night, the great Lobster ball was taking place. Lobsters came from far and wide, dancing and merry making, but the lobster Princess refused to join in, choosing instead to sit by her father's side, inconsolable. Suddenly the doors burst open, and Declan the crab strode in. The Lobsters all stopped their dancing, the Princess gasped and the King Lobster rose from his throne.

Slowly, painstakingly, Declan the crab made his way across the floor... and all could see that he was walking, not sideways, but FORWARDS, one claw after another! Step by step he made his approach towards the throne, until he finally looked King lobster in the eye.

There was a deadly hush...

Finally, the crab spoke...

"F*ck, I'm pissed."

SUBJECT: LAWS

Many laws have been formulated over the years. There are several books that quote various laws, here's a few you might like:

ANTHONY'S WORKSHOP LAW:
Any tool, when dropped, always rolls into the most inaccessible corner of the workshop.

COROLLARY:
On the way to the corner, any dropped tool will always fall on your toe.

BOREN'S LAWS:
1. When in doubt, mumble
2. When in trouble, delegate
3. When in charge, ponder.

THE CHRISTMAS PRESENTS LAWS:
1. If it doesn't run off the mains, batteries are never included
2. If it does run off the mains, a plug is never included
3. Everything is designed to break by Dec 26
4. If you can wear it, it's the wrong size
5. If it fits, the colour is never right

CLAY'S CONCLUSION
Creativity is great, but plagiarism is faster.

DONOHUE'S LAW
If a thing's worth doing make sure you do it for money.

GARDENING LAWS
1. The rake you step on is always teeth up, so not only does it injure your foot, but it also smacks you in the mouth with the handle.
2. Other people's tools only work in other people's gardens.
3. Gimmicky devices don't works.
4. You get the most flowers or vegetables of the sort that you need the least.
5. It always rains after you've watered the lawn
6. If you've spent days planning to have a bonfire or a barbecue, when you finally light it, all your neighbours decide to hang out their washing.

JOHN'S COLLATERAL COROLLARY
In order to get a loan, you must first prove that you don't need it.

JONES' LAW
The man who can smile when things are going wrong, has just thought of someone he can blame it on.

LEWANDOWSKI'S AIR–TURBULENCE PRINCIPLE
An airline flight will remain smooth until meal and/or drinks service begins. A smooth flight will resume when meal and/or drinks service ends.

THE MONEY MAXIM
Money isn't everything – for one thing, it isn't plentiful.

PALMER'S LAW
The only thing better than a lie is a true story that no one will believe.

ROSE'S LAW OF INVESTMENT
Never invest in anything that has to be painted or fed.

SWARTZ'S MAXIM
Live every day as if it were your last, and one day you'll be right.

VARGAS'S LAWS
1. If directions to a place include the words 'you can't miss it', you will.
2. There is no such thing as a little garlic – or a mild heart attack – or a few children.
3. A jar that cannot be opened by any combination of house– hold tools, force and determination, will instantly open if picked up by the lid.

WEILER'S LAW
Nothing is impossible for the man who doesn't have to do it himself.

SUBJECT: LITTLE JIMMY

For his birthday Little Jimmy asked for a mountain bike.

His father said, "Son, we'd love to give you one but the bond on this house is $400,000 and your mother just lost her job. There's no way we can afford it right now." The next day the father saw Little Jimmy heading out the front door with a suitcase. So he asked, "Son, where are you going?"

Little Jimmy told him, "I was walking past your room last night and I heard you tell Mum that you were pulling out. Then I heard her tell you to wait, because she was coming, too. And I'll be damned if I'm sticking around here by myself with a $400,000 bond and no bike!"

SUBJECT: LOW DOWN

A guy walks into a psychiatrist's office wearing Glad Wrap.

The psychiatrist says, "Well, I can see your nuts".

SUBJECT: LAUGH, TO KEEP YOU GOING THROUGH THE WEEK!

There were three good arguments that Jesus was Black:
1. He called everyone brother.
2. He liked Gospel.
3. He couldn't get a fair trial.

But then there were three equally good arguments that Jesus was Jewish:
1. He went into His Father's business.
2. He lived at home until he was 33.
3. He was sure his Mother was a virgin and his Mother was sure He was God.

But then there were three equally good arguments that Jesus was Italian:
1. He talked with His hands.
2. He had wine with His meals.
3. He used olive oil.

But then there were three equally good arguments that Jesus was a Californian:
1. He never cut His hair.
2. He walked around barefoot all the time.
3. He started a new religion.

But then there were three equally good arguments that Jesus was an American Indian:
1. He was at peace with nature.
2. He ate a lot of fish.
3. He talked about the Great Spirit.

But then there were three equally good arguments the Jesus was Irish:
1. He never got married.
2. He was always telling stories.
3. He loved green pastures.

But the most compelling evidence of all – three proofs that Jesus was a woman:
1. He fed a crowd at a moment's notice when there was no food.
2. He kept trying to get a message across to a bunch of men who just didn't get it.
3. And even when He was dead, He had to get up because there was work to do.

AMEN

SUBJECT: GOT TO LAUGH

Carnivorous lizard sets back toddler's toilet training

Potty training is difficult enough for any toddler but one youngster has suffered a particularly dramatic experience after a carnivorous lizard emerged from the family toilet while he was using it.

The boy's mother discovered the 75 centimetre Teju lizard, a carnivorous variety from South America, as she helped her three-year-old use the toilet, the Bergen aquarium in Western Norway says.

The black, yellow-banded lizard weighed 1.5 kilograms.

"If it had the opportunity, I'm sure that it would have planted its teeth in anything that presented itself," Kees Ekeli, the head of the aquarium, which rounded up the reptile, told AFP.

"The little boy was learning to use the toilet rather than diapers and one might say that his training has suffered a serious setback," he said.

SUBJECT: LEFT FOOTER'S DICTIONARY

AMEN (a-men). Only part of a prayer that everyone knows.

HOLY WATER n. A liquid whose chemical formulae is H20LY.

INCENSE (in-sens) n. Holy Smoke.

RECESSIONAL (ri-seshé-nel) adj. The ceremonial procession at the end of Mass, led by parishioners trying to beat the crowd to the parking lot.

SUBJECT: LEPRECHAUN

An American golfer playing in Ireland hooked his drive into the woods.

Looking for his ball, he found a little Leprechaun flat on his back, a big bump on his head and the golfer's ball beside him. Horrified, the golfer got his water bottle from the cart and poured it over the little guy, reviving him. "Arrgh! What happened?" the Leprechaun asked. "I'm afraid I hit you with my golf ball," the golfer says. "Oh, I see. Well, ye got me fair and square. Ye get three wishes, so whaddya want?" "Thank God, you're all right!" the golfer answers in relief. "I don't want anything. I'm just glad you're OK and I apologise." And the golfer walked off.

"What a nice guy," the Leprechaun says to himself. I have to do something for him. I'll give him the three things I would want – a great golf game, all the money he ever needs and a fantastic sex life."

A year goes by and the American golfer is back. On the same hole, he again hits a bad drive into the woods and the Leprechaun is there waiting for him. "'Twas me that made ye hit the ball here," the little guy says. "I just want to ask ye, how's yer golf game?" "My game is fantastic!" the golfer answers. I'm an internationally famous golfer now." He adds, "By the way, it's good to see you. Are you all right?" "Oh, I'm fine now, thank ye."

"I did that fer yer golf game, you know. And tell me, how's yer money situation?" "Why, it's just wonderful!" the golfer states. "When I need cash, I just reach in my pocket and pull out $100 bills I didn't even know were there!" "I did that fer ye also. And tell me, how's yer sex life?" The golfer blushes, turns his head away in embarrassment and says shyly, "It's OK." "C'mon, c'mon now," urged the Leprechaun, "I'm wanting to know if I did a good job. How many times a week?" Blushing even more, the golfer looks around then whispers, "Once, sometimes twice a week." "What??" responds the Leprechaun in shock. "That's all? Only once or twice a week?" "Well," says the golfer, "I figure that's not bad for a Catholic priest in a small parish."

SUBJECT: LOOKING AFTER MUM

Four brothers left home for college, and they became successful doctors and lawyers and prospered. Some years later, they chatted after having dinner together. They discussed the gifts they were able to give their elderly mother who lived far away in another city.

The first said, "I had a big house built for Mama."

The second said, "I had a hundred thousand dollar theatre built in the house."

The third said, "I had my Mercedes dealer deliver an SL600 to her."

The fourth said, "You know how Mamma loved reading the Bible, and you know she can't read any more because she can't see very well. I met this preacher who told me about a parrot that can recite the entire bible. It took twenty preachers 12 years to teach him. I had to pledge to contribute $100,000 a year for twenty years to the church, but it was worth it. Mamma just has to name the chapter and verse and the parrot will recite it."

The other brothers were impressed. After the holidays Mum sent out her thank you notes.

She wrote:
"Milton, the house you built is so huge I live in only one room, but I have to clean the whole house. Thanks anyway."

"Marvin, I am too old to travel. I stay home, I have my groceries delivered, so I never use the Mercedes. The thought was good. Thanks."

"Michael, you gave me an expensive theatre with Dolby sound, it could hold 50 people, but all of my friends are dead, I've lost my hearing and I'm nearly blind. I'll never use it. Thank you for the gesture, just the same."

"Dearest Melvin, you were the only son to have the good sense to give a little thought to your gift. The chicken was delicious. Thank you."

Love, Mama

SUBJECT: THE LOVER

Becky was in bed with her lover when she heard her husband opening the front door.

"Hurry." she said, "stand in the corner." The Becky quickly rubbed baby oil all over him and then dusted him with talcum powder.

"Don't move until I tell you to," she whispered. "Just pretend you're a statue."

"What's this, honey?" her husband inquired as he entered the room.

"OH, it's a statue," Becky nonchalantly.

"The Smiths bought one for their bedroom. I liked it so much, I got one for us too."

No more was said about the statue, not even later when they went to sleep.

Around two in the morning, the husband got out of bed, went to the kitchen and returned a while later with a sandwich and a glass of milk.

"Here," he said to the statue, "eat something. I stood like an idiot at the Smiths for three days and nobody offered me as much as a glass of water."

SUBJECT: LIQUID MEAL

Avoid drink driving. Freeze the beer and then eat it.

SUBJECT: LITTLE MELISSA

Little Melissa comes home from first grade and tells her father that they learned about the history of Valentine's Day.

"Since Valentine's Day is for a Christian saint, and we're Jewish," she asks, "will God get mad at me for giving someone a valentine?"

Melissa's father thinks a bit, then says, "No, I don't think God would get mad, who do you want to give a Valentine to?" "Osama Bin Laden," she says.

"Why Osama Bin Laden," her father asks in shock.

"Well," she says, "I thought that if a little American Jewish girl could have enough love to give Osama a Valentine, he might start to think that maybe we're not all bad, and maybe start loving people a little bit. And if other kids saw what I did and sent Valentines to Osama, he'd love everyone a lot. And then he'd start going all over the place to tell everyone how much he loved them and how he didn't hate anyone any more."

Her father's heart swells and he looks at his daughter with new found pride. "Melissa, that's the most wonderful thing I've ever heard."

"I know," Melissa says, "and once that gets him out in the open, the Marines could shoot the prick."

SUBJECT: LITTLE WONDER

There was a man who entered a local newspaper's pun contest. He sent in ten puns in the hope that at least one would win.

Unfortunately, no pun in ten did.

SUBJECT: LATEX GLOVES

A dentist noticed that his next patient, an elderly lady, was looking very nervous so he decided to tell her a little joke as he put on his gloves. "Do you know how they make these gloves?" he asked.

"No, I don't" she replied.

"Well," he spoofed, "there's a building in China with a big tank of latex. Workers of all hand sizes walk up to the tank, dip in their hands, let them dry, then peel off the gloves and throw them into boxes of the right size."

She didn't crack a smile. "Oh well, I tried," he thought.

But five minutes later, during a delicate portion of the dental procedure, she burst out laughing.

"What's so funny?" he asked.

"I was just picturing how condoms are made!" she said.

Gotta watch those little old ladies! Their minds are always working...

SUBJECT: LITTLE FOLK

An honest seven year old admitted calmly to her parents that Billy has kissed her after class.

"How did that happen?" gasped the mum.

"It wasn't easy," admitted the girl, "but three friends helped me catch him."

SUBJECT: MARTHA STEWART

"Right here on CBS there's a new reality show to find the next Martha Stewart. Why? Because America can't go five months without a domestic diva. On the show they have all kinds of Martha Stewart type challenges. Tonight they had a shower room cat fight."

– Dave Letterman

SUBJECT: SPECIAL MOMENTS

The children had all been photographed and the teacher was trying to persuade them each to buy a copy of the group photo.

"Just think in years to come you will be able to look back and think, 'there's Lynnette, she's now a lawyer. There's Billy, he's now a doctor.'"

And from the back of the class room,
"Look there's the teacher, she's dead."

SUBJECT: THE SECRET OF A HAPPY MARRIAGE

My wife and I have the secret of making a marriage last:
Two times a week, we go to a nice restaurant, have a little wine,
some good food and companionship.

She goes Tuesday, I go Friday.

We also sleep in separate beds, hers in Sydney mine in Melbourne.

I take my wife everywhere, but she keeps finding her way back.

I asked my wife where she wanted to go for Anniversary,
"Somewhere I haven't been in a long time" she said, so I suggested
the kitchen.

We always hold hands... If I let go she shops.

She has an electric blender, electric toaster, and electric bread maker,
then she said, "There are too many gadgets and no place to sit down"
so I bought her an electric chair.

Remember marriage is the number one cause of divorce.

Statistically, 100 per cent of all divorces started with marriage.

I haven't spoken to my wife for about 18 months, I don't like to
interrupt her.

The last fight was my fault, my wife asked, "What's on TV?"
I said, "Dust."

SUBJECT: MALE MATESHIP
VERSES FEMALE FRIENDSHIP

Friendship among women:

A woman doesn't come home at night. The next day she tells her husband that she slept over at a friend's house. The man calls his wife's ten best friends. None of them know about it.

Mateship among men:

A man doesn't come home at night. The next day he tells his wife that he slept over at a mate's house. The woman calls her husband's ten best mates. Eight of them say he did sleep over and two claim he's still there.

SUBJECT: MAGIC BUMPER STICKERS

- Constipated people don't give a crap.
- Practice safe sex: go screw yourself.
- Accidents cause people.
- Impotence; nature's way of saying 'no hard feelings'.
- You're just jealous because the voices are talking to me.
- If we quit voting will they all go away?
- Money isn't everything but it sure keeps the kids in touch.
- Don't be sexist - chicks hate it.

SUBJECT: GETTING MARRIED

A lonely woman, aged 70, decided that it was time to get married.

She put an ad in the local paper that read:

"HUSBAND WANTED! MUST BE IN MY AGE GROUP (70s), MUST NOT BEAT ME, MUST NOT RUN AROUND ON ME AND MUST STILL BE GOOD IN BED!
ALL APPLICANTS PLEASE APPLY IN PERSON."

On the second day she heard the doorbell. Much to her dismay, she opened the door to see a grey-haired gentleman sitting in a wheel chair.

He had no arms or legs.

The old woman said, "You're not really asking me to consider you, are you?"

"Just look at you... you have no legs!"

The old man smiled, "Therefore I cannot run around on you!"

She snorted. "You don't have any hands either!"

Again the old man smiled, "Nor can I beat you!"

She raised an eyebrow and gazed intently. "Are you still good in bed?"

With that, the old gentleman leaned back, beamed a big broad smile and said, "I rang the doorbell didn't I?"

SUBJECT: THE MONK

A man is driving down the road and breaks down near a monastery.

He goes to the monastery, knocks on the door, and says, "My car broke down. Do you think I could stay the night?" The monks raucously accept him, feed him dinner, even fix his car. As the man tries to fall asleep, he hears a strange yet wonderful sound. A sound unlike anything he's ever heard before.

The Sirens that nearly seduced Odysseus comes to his mind. He doesn't sleep that night. He tosses and turns trying to figure out what could possibly be making such a seductive sound.

The next morning, he asks the monks what the sound was, but they say, "We can't tell you. You're not a monk."

Distraught, the man is forced to leave.

Years later, after never being able to forget that sound, the man goes back to the monastery and pleads for the answer again.

The monks reply, "We can't tell you. You're not a monk."

The man says, "If the only way I can find out what is making that beautiful sound is to become a monk, then please, make me a monk."

The monks reply, "You must travel the earth and tell us how many blades of grass there are and the exact number of grains of sand When you find these answers, you will have become a monk."

The man sets about his task. After years of searching he returns and knocks on the door of the monastery.

"I have travelled the earth and have found what you have asked for: By design, the world is in a state of perpetual change. Only God knows what you ask. All a man can know is himself, and only then if he is honest and reflective and willing to strip away self deception."

The monks reply, "Congratulations. You are now a monk. We shall now show you the source of the mystery sound."

The monks lead the man to a wooden door, where the head monk says, "The sound is beyond that door." The monks give him the key, and he opens the door. Behind the wooden door is another door made of stone. The man is given the key to the stone door and he opens it, only to find a door made of ruby. And so it went on that he needed keys to doors of emerald, gold and diamond.

Finally, the monks say, "This is the last key to the last door." The man is apprehensive to no end. His life's wish is behind the door! He unlocks the door, turns the knob, and behind that door he is utterly amazed to find the source of that haunting and seductive sound...

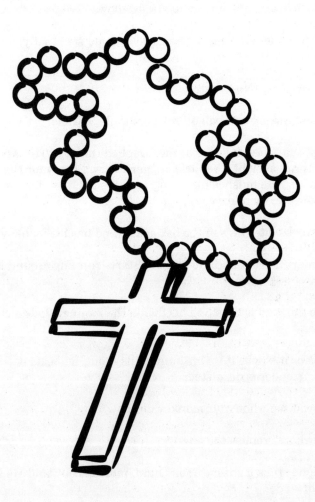

But I can't tell you what it is because you're not a monk!

SUBJECT: MAKING SURE...

A guy walks into a bar with his pet monkey. He orders a drink and while he's drinking the monkey jumps all around the place.

The monkey grabs some olives off the bar and eats them, then grabs some sliced limes and eats them, then jumps onto the pool table, grabs one of the billiard balls, sticks it in his mouth, and to everyone's amazement, somehow swallows it whole.

The bartender screams at the guy, "Did you see what your monkey just did?"

The guy says, "No, what?"

"He just ate the cue ball off my pool table... whole!"

"Yeah, that doesn't surprise me," replied the guy, "He eats everything in sight, the little bugger. Sorry. I'll pay for the cue ball and stuff." He finishes his drink, pays his bill, pays for the stuff the monkey ate, then leaves.

Two weeks later he's in the bar again, and has his monkey with him.

He orders a drink and the monkey starts running around the bar again.

While the man is finishing his drink, the monkey finds a cherry on the bar.

He grabs it, sticks it up his bum, pulls it out, and eats it.
The bartender is disgusted.

"Did you see what your monkey did now?"

"No, what?" replies the guy.

"Well, he stuck a cherry up his bum, pulled it out, and ate it!" said the bartender."

"Yeah, that doesn't surprise me," replied the guy. "He still eats everything in sight, but ever since the cue ball incident, he measures everything first."

SUBJECT: THE MINISTER

The Minister from a small country town is driving to the city and gets stopped for speeding on the Highway. The policeman smells a tinge of alcohol on the driver's breath and then sees an empty wine bottle on the floor of the car.

He says, "Sir have you been drinking?"
"Just water" says the minister.
The policeman says, "Then why do I smell wine?"

The minister looks at the bottle and says, "Good Lord! He's done it again!"

SUBJECT: MOTTOS

- A day without sunshine is like night.
- I got lost in thought. It was unfamiliar territory.
- I feel like I am diagonally parked in a parallel universe.
- Honk if you like peace and quiet.
- I drive way too fast to worry about cholesterol.
- Support bacteria, they are the only culture some people have.
- I intend to live forever - so far, so good.

SUBJECT: MORALS

A teacher gave her class of 11-year-olds an assignment:
Get their parents to tell them a story with a moral at the end of it.

The next day the kids came back and one by one began to tell their stories.

Ashley said, "My father's a farmer and we have a lot of egg laying hens. One time we were taking our eggs to market in a basket on the front seat of the car when we hit a big bump in the road and all the eggs went flying and broke and made a mess."

"What's the moral of the story?" asked the teacher.

"Don't put all your eggs in one basket!"

"Very good," said the teacher.

Next little Sarah raised her hand and said, "Our family are farmers too, but we raise chickens for the meat market. One day we had a dozen eggs, but when they hatched we only got ten live chicks, and the moral to this story is, 'Don't count your chickens before they're hatched'."

"That was a fine story Sarah. Michael, do you have a story to share?"

"Yes. My daddy told me this story about my Aunt Karen. Aunt Karen was a flight engineer on a plane in the Gulf War and the plane got hit. She had to bail out over enemy territory and all she had was a bottle of whisky, a machine gun and a machete. She drank the whisky on the way down so it wouldn't break and then she landed right in the middle of 100 enemy troops. She killed seventy of them with the machine gun until she ran out of bullets. Then she killed twenty more with the machete until the blade broke.
And then she killed the last ten with her bare hands."

"Good heavens," said the horrified teacher, "what kind of moral did your daddy tell you from that horrible story?"

"Stay the f*ck away from Aunt Karen when she's been drinking."

SUBJECT: MARRIAGE

A dinner conversation that took the wrong turn:

WIFE:	"What would you do if I died? Would you get married again?"
HUSBAND:	"Definitely not!"

WIFE:	"Why not – don't you like being married?"
HUSBAND:	"Of course I do."

WIFE:	"Then why wouldn't you remarry?"
HUSBAND:	"Okay, I'd get married again."

WIFE:	"You would?" (with a hurtful look on her face)
HUSBAND:	(makes audible groan).

WIFE:	"Would you sleep with her in our bed?"
HUSBAND:	"Where else would we sleep?"

WIFE:	"Would you replace my pictures with hers?"
HUSBAND:	"That would seem like the proper thing to do."

WIFE:	"Would she wear my jewellery?"
HUSBAND:	"Well, I suppose so."

WIFE:	"Would she use my golf clubs?"
HUSBAND:	"No, she's left-handed."

WIFE:	– – – silence – – –
HUSBAND:	"Shit ..."

SUBJECT: SMART MALE

An accountant gets home late one night and his wife says , "Where in the hell have you been?" He replies, "I was out getting a tattoo."

"A tattoo?" she frowned. "What kind of tattoo did you get?"
"I got a hundred dollar bill tattooed on my privates," he said proudly.

"What the hell were you thinking?" she said, shaking her head in disdain.

"Why on earth would an accountant get a hundred dollar bill tattooed on his privates?"

"Well, one, I like to watch my money grow."

"Two, once in awhile I like to play with my money."

"Three, I like how money feels in my hand, and finally, instead of you going out shopping, you can stay right here at home and blow a hundred bucks any time you want!!!"

SUBJECT: MURPHY'S TECHNOLOGY LAWS

1. You can never tell which way the train went by looking at the track.

2. Logic is a systematic method of coming to the wrong conclusion with confidence.

3. Technology is dominated by those who manage what they do not understand.

4. If builders built buildings the way programmers wrote programs, then the first woodpecker that came along would destroy civilization.

5. An expert is one who knows more and more about less and less until he/she knows absolutely everything about nothing.

6. Tell a man there are 300 billion stars in the universe, and he'll believe you. Tell him a bench has wet paint on it, and he'll have to touch to be sure.

7. All great discoveries are made by mistake.

8. Nothing ever gets built on schedule or within budget.

9. All's well that ends... period.

10. A meeting is an event at which minutes are kept and hours are lost.

SUBJECT: MAKING SURE

A man goes to see Mel Gibson's new movie, The Passion of Christ. He is inspired to take his family to Israel to see the places where Jesus lived and died.

While on vacation his mother-in-law dies. An undertaker in Tel Aviv explains that they can ship the body home to Wisconsin at a cost of $10,000 or the mother-in-law could be buried in Israel for $500 US.

The man says, "We'll ship her home."

The undertaker asks, "Are you sure? That's an awfully big Expense and we can do a very nice burial here."

The man says, "Look, 2000 years ago they buried a guy here and three days later he rose from the dead... I just can't take that chance."

SUBJECT: MAGIC KINGDOM

Snow White saw Pinocchio in the woods.

She ran up to him, pushed him, and he fell falt on his back.

She sat on his face crying, "Lie to me. Lie to me."

SUBJECT: THREE TOUGH MICE

Three mice are sitting at a bar in a pretty rough neighbourhood late at night trying to impress each other about how tough they are.

The first mouse throws down a shot of bourbon, slams the empty glass onto the bar, turns to the second mouse and says, "When I see a mousetrap, I lay on my back and set it off with my foot. When the bar comes down, I catch it in my teeth, bench press it twenty times to work up an appetite, and then make off with the cheese."

The second mouse orders up two shots of tequila, drinks them down one after the other, slams both glasses onto the bar, turns to the first mouse and replies, "Oh yeah? When I see rat poison, I collect as much as I can, take it home, grind it up to a powder, and add it to my coffee each morning so I can get a good buzz going for the rest of the day." The two then turn to the third mouse.

The third mouse finishes the beer he has in front of him, lets out a long sigh and says to the first two, "I don't have time for this bullshit. Gotta go home and have sex with the cat."

SUBJECT: MEN ARE JUST HAPPY PEOPLE

Men Are Just Happy People – what do you expect from such simple creatures?

Your last name stays put.
The garage is all yours.
Wedding plans take care of themselves.
Chocolate is just another snack.
You can be President.
You can never be pregnant.
You can wear a white t-shirt to a water park.
You can wear NO shirt to a water park.
Car mechanics tell you the truth.
The world is your urinal.
You never have to drive to another gas station rest room because this one is just too icky.
You don't have to stop and think of which way to turn a nut on a bolt.
Same work, more pay.
Wrinkles add character.
Wedding dress $5000. Tux rental $100.
People never stare at your chest when you're talking to them.
The occasional well-rendered belch is practically expected.
New shoes don't cut, blister, or mangle your feet.
One mood all the time.
A five day vacation requires only one suitcase.
You can open all your own jars.
You get extra credit for the slightest act of thoughtfulness.
If someone forgets to invite you, he or she can still be your friend.
Your underwear is $8.95 for a three pack.
Three pairs of shoes are more than enough.
You almost never have strap problems in public.
You are unable to see wrinkles in your clothes.
The same hairstyle lasts for years, maybe decades.
You only have to shave your face and neck.
You can play with toys all your life.
One wallet and one pair of shoes one colour for all seasons.
You can wear shorts no matter how your legs look.
You can 'do' your nails with a pocket knife.
You have freedom of choice concerning growing a mustache.
You can do Christmas shopping for 25 relatives on December 24 in 25 minutes.

SUBJECT: MEMORABLE MOMENTS IN MUSIC

The Ten Top Country Western Songs:

10. I Hate Every Bone In Her Body But Mine

9. How Can I Miss You If You Won't Go Away?

8. I Still Miss You Baby, but My Aim's Getting Better

7. I Wouldn't Take Her to A Dog Fight 'Cause I'm Afraid She'd Win

6. I'll marry You Tomorrow but Let's Honeymoon Tonight

5. My wife Ran off with My Best Friend and I Sure Do Miss Him

4. You're The Reason Our Kids Are So Ugly

3. Her Teeth Was Stained But Her Heart Was Pure

2. She's Looking Better After Every Beer

And the Number One song is ..

1. I Ain't Never Gone To Bed With an Ugly Woman... But I've Sure Woke Up with a few.

SUBJECT: MORNING MOMENTS

"You know Honey," the little onle lady said, "my nipples are as hot for you today as they were 50 years ago."

"I'm not surprised," said gramps. "One is in your coffee and one is in your porridge."

SUBJECT: IF MICROSOFT MADE CARS

For all us who feel only the deepest love and affection for the way computers have enhanced our lives, read on.

At Comdex recently, Bill Gates reportedly compared the computer industry with the Auto industry and stated, "If GM had kept up with the technology like the computer industry has, we would be driving $25 cars, that got 1,000 miles to the gallon."

In response to Bill's comments, General Motors issued a press release stating:

If GM had developed technology like Microsoft, we would be driving cars with the following characteristics.

1. For no reason whatsoever, your car would crash twice a day.

2. Every time they repainted the lines in the road, you would have to buy a new car.

3. Occasionally your car would die on the freeway for no reason.

4. You would have to pull over to the side of the road, close all the windows, shut off the car, restart it, and reopen the windows before you could continue. For some reason you would simply accept this.

5. Occasionally, executing a manoeuvre such as a left turn would cause your car to shut down and refuse to restart, in which case you would have to reinstall the engine.

6. Macintosh would make a car that was powered by the sun, was reliable, five times as fast and twice as easy to drive, but would run on only five percent of the roads.

7. The oil, water temperature, and alternator warning lights would all be replaced by a single 'This car has performed an illegal operation' warning light.

8. The air bag system would ask, 'Are you sure?' before deploying.

9. Occasionally, for no reason whatsoever, your car would lock you out and refuse to let you in until you simultaneously lifted the door handle, turned the key and grabbed hold of the radio antenna.

10. Every time a new car was introduced, car buyers would have to learn how to drive all over again, because none off the controls would operate in the same manner as the old car.

11. Oh yeah, and last but not least... you'd have to press the 'Start' button to turn the engine off.

SUBJECT: MYSTERIOUS SIGNS...

Did I read that sign right?

TOILET OUT OF ORDER. PLEASE USE FLOOR BELOW

In a London department store:
BARGAIN BASEMENT UPSTAIRS

In an office:
WOULD THE PERSON WHO TOOK THE STEP LADDER
YESTERDAY PLEASE BRING IT BACK OR FURTHER STEPS
WILL BE TAKEN

In an office:
AFTER TEA BREAK STAFF SHOULD EMPTY THE TEAPOT
AND STAND UPSIDE DOWN ON THE DRAINING BOARD

Outside a second-hand shop:
WE EXCHANGE ANYTHING – BICYCLES, WASHING
MACHINES, ETC. WHY NOT BRING YOUR WIFE ALONG AND
GET A WONDERFUL BARGAIN?

Notice in health food shop window:
CLOSED DUE TO ILLNESS

Spotted in a safari park:
ELEPHANTS PLEASE STAY IN YOUR CAR

Seen during a conference:
FOR ANYONE WHO HAS CHILDREN AND DOESN'T KNOW IT,
THERE IS A DAY CARE ON THE FIRST FLOOR

Notice in a farmer's field:
THE FARMER ALLOWS WALKERS TO CROSS THE FIELD FOR
FREE, BUT THE BULL CHARGES.

Message on a leaflet:
IF YOU CANNOT READ, THIS LEAFLET WILL TELL YOU HOW
TO GET LESSONS

On a repair shop door:
WE CAN REPAIR ANYTHING. PLEASE KNOCK HARD ON THE
DOOR – THE BELL DOESN'T WORK

SUBJECT: NUMBERS

Donald Rumsfeld is giving the president his daily briefing.

He concludes by saying, "Yesterday, three Brazilian soldiers were killed in an accident.

"OH NO!" the President exclaims. "That's terrible!"

His staff sits stunned at this display of emotion, nervously watching as the president sits, head in hands.

Finally, the President looks up and asks...

"How many is a Brazilian ??!"

SUBJECT: NATURAL LAW

DICTATORSHIP: You have 2 cows. The government takes both and shoots you.

PURE DEMOCRACY: You have two cows. Your neighbours decide who gets the milk.

REPRESENTATIVE DEMOCRACY: You have two cows. Through voting, your neighbours decide who gets the milk.

BRITISH DEMOCRACY: You have two cows, you feed them sheep brains, they go mad, the government doesn't do anything.

BUREAUCRACY: You have two cows. At first the government regulates what you can feed them and when you can milk them. Then it pays you not to milk them. After that, the government takes both, shoots one, milks the other, pours the milk down the sink. Then it requires you to fill out a form to account for the missing cow.

SUBJECT: NINE KIDS

Husband and wife are waiting at the bus stop with their nine children. A blind man joins them after a few minutes. When the bus arrives, they find it overloaded and only the wife and the nine kids are able to fit onto the bus.

So the husband and the blind man decide to walk. After a while, the husband gets irritated by the ticking of the stick of the blind man as he taps it on the side walk, and says to him, "Why don't you put a piece of rubber at the end of your stick? That ticking sound is driving me crazy."

The blind man replies, "If you would've put a rubber at the end of YOUR stick, we'd be riding the bus... so shut the hell up."

SUBJECT: PHRASES FOR YOUR 'OUT-OF-OFFICE AUTO EMAIL REPLY'

I am currently out at a job interview and will reply to you if I fail to get the position. Be prepared for my mood.

I'm not really out of the office. I'm just ignoring you.

You are receiving this automatic notification because I am out of the office. If I was in, chances are you wouldn't have received anything at all.

Sorry to have missed you but I am at the doctors having my brain removed so that I may be promoted to management.

I will be unable to delete all the unread, worthless emails you send me until I return from vacation on 18/4. Please be patient and your mail will be deleted in the order it was received.

Thank you for your email. Your credit card has been charged $5.99 for the first ten words and $1.99 for each additional word in your message.

The email server is unable to verify your server connection and is unable to deliver this message. Please restart your computer and try sending again. The beauty of it is that when I return, I can see how many in-duh-vidual did this over and over.

Thank you for your message, which has been added to a queuing system.

You are currently in 352nd place, and can expect to receive a reply in approximately 19 weeks.

I've run away to join a different circus.

AND, FINALLY, ABSOLUTELY THE BEST:

I will be out of the office for the next two weeks for medical reasons. When I return, please refer to me as 'Loretta' instead of 'Steve'.

SUBJECT: THE OPERATION

The patient, well known for his grumpiness, awakened after the operation to find himself in a room with all the blinds all drawn.

"Why are all the blinds closed, Nurse?" he asked.

"Well." the nurse responded, "They're fighting a huge fire across the street, and we didn't want you to wake up and think the operation had failed."

SUBJECT: OH DEAR!

A man is in a hotel lobby.

He wants to ask the clerk a question, but as he turns to go to the front desk, he accidently bumps into a woman beside him. As he does so his elbow goes into her breasts.

They are both startled and he says, "Madam, if your heart is as soft as your breast, I know you'll forgive me."

She replies, "If your penis is as hard as your elbow, I'm in room 1221."

SUBJECT: COUNTRY OF ORIGIN

The Italian says, "I'm tired and thirsty. I must have wine."

The Mexican says, "I'm tired and thirsty. I must have tequila."

The Scot says, "I'm tired and thirsty. I must have scotch."

The Swede says, "I'm tired and thirsty. I must have aquavit."

The Japanese says, "I'm tired and thirsty. I must have sake."

The Russian says, "I'm tired and thirsty. I must have vodka."

The German says, "I'm tired and thirsty. I must have beer."

The Greek says, "I'm tired and thirsty. I must have ouzo."

The Jew says, "I'm tired and thirsty. I must have diabetes."

SUBJECT: ONE LINERS...

Q: How do you get holy water?
A: Boil the hell out of it.

Q: What did the fish say when it hit a concrete wall?
A: Dam!

Q: What's the definition of mixed emotions?
A: When you see your mother-in-law backing off a cliff in your new car.

Q: What is a zebra?
A: An undergarment that is 26 sizes larger than an 'A' bra.

SUBJECT: OOPS...

This guy was lonely and so he decided life would be more fun if he had a pet. So he went to the pet shop and told the owner that he wanted to buy an unusual pet.

After some discussion, he finally bought a centipede which came in little white box to use for his house.

He took the box back home, found a good location for the box, and decided he would start off by taking his new pet to the pub to have a drink.

So he asked the centipede in the box, "Would you like to go down to The Queen's Head with me and have a beer?" But there was no answer from his new pet.

This bothered him a bit, but he waited a few minutes and then asked him again, "How about going to the pub for a drink?"

But again, there was no answer from his new friend and pet. So he waited a few minutes more, thinking about the situation. He decided to ask him one more time. This time, putting his face up against the centipede's house and shouting, "Hey, in there! Would you like to go to The Queen's Head and have a drink with me?"

Scroll down!!!!!!!!!!!! YOU ARE GOING TO LOVE THIS!

A little voice came out of the box:...

"I heard you the first time! I'm putting my f*cking shoes on."

P

SUBJECT: ST. PATRICK'S DAY HUMOUR

Three men, one American, one Japanese and an Irishman were sitting naked in a sauna.

Suddenly there was a beeping sound. The American pressed his forearm and the beep stopped.

The others looked at him questioningly. "That was my pager," he said, "I have a microchip under the skin of my arm."

A few minutes later a phone rang. The Japanese fellow lifted his palm to his ear. When he finished he explained, "That was my mobile phone. I have a microchip in my hand."

The Irishman felt decidedly low-tech, but not to be outdone he decided he had to do something just as impressive. He stepped out of the sauna and went to the bathroom. He returned with a piece of toilet paper hanging from his butt. The others raised their eyebrows and stared at him.

The Irishman glanced around behind in and said ... Oh my , will you look at that, I'm getting a fax"

SUBJECT: PRAYERFUL

A nun asked her young class if they knew why it was important to be quiet during Mass.

A small voice said, "Because people are sleeping."

SUBJECT: PHRASES

If you ever travelling in the Middle East, you may find it useful to know these simple phrases. With deep respect to the Islam nation, be it known that less than two per cent of the population belong to radical extremist factions. Most Muslims are of course, very nice people...

AKBAR KHALI-KILI HAFTIR LOTFAN.
Thank you for showing me your marvellous gun.

FEKR GABUL CRADAN DAVAT PAEH GUSH DIVAR.
I am delighted to accept your kind invitation to lie on the floor with my arms above my head and my legs apart.

SHOMAEH FEKR TAMOMEH OEH GOFTEH BANDE.
I agree with everything you have ever said or thought in your life.

AUTO ARREREGH DAVATEMAN MANO SEPAHEH HAST.
It is exceptionally kind of you to allow me to travel in the boot of your car.

FASHAL-EH TUPEHMAN NA DEGAT MANO GOFTAM
CHEESHAYEH MOHEMARA EHKESH VAREHMAN.
If you will do me the kindness of not harming my genitals, I will gladly reciprocate by betraying my country in public.

KHREL JEPAHEH MANEH VA JAYEH AMERIKAHEY.
I will tell you the names and addresses of many Australian spies travelling as aid workers.

BALLI, BALLI, BALLI !
Whatever you say!

MATERNIER GHERMEZ AHLEIEH, GHORBAN.
The red blindfold will be lovely, excellency.

TIEKH NUNEH OB KHRELEH BEZORG VA KHRUBE BOYAST INO
BEGERAM.
The water soaked bread crumbs are delicious, thank you. I must get the recipe.

EY ASHTEC JEZERINEH GAHUL SALMAN RUSHDIE
I completely agree. Salman Rushdie is an arsehole.

SUBJECT:PENSIONERS SEX

Two old pensioners are taking a trip down memory lane, by going back to where they first met.

Sitting at the café, the little old man says, "Remember the first time I met you 50 years ago?" We left this café, went around the corner behind the gas works, and I gave you one from behind."

"Why yes, I remember it well dear," replies the little old lady with a smile. "Well for old time's sake, lets go there again. And I'll give you one from behind."

The two pensioners pay their bill and leave the café. The young man sitting behind them, overheard the conversation and smiles to himself, thinking it would be quite amusing to see two old pensioners at it. He gets up and follows them. Sure enough, he sees the two pensioners near the gas works. The little old lady pulls of her knickers and lifts her dress.

The old man pulls down his pants and grabs the lady's hips, and the little old lady reaches over for the fence. Well, what follows is 40 minutes of the most furious sex the man has ever seen. The little old man is banging away at the woman at a pace that could only be describes as phenomenal. Limbs are going every where, the movement is a blur, and they don't stop for a single breath. Finally, they collapse and don't move for an hour.

Well, the man is stunned. Never in his life has he ever seen anything that equals to this... not in the movies, not from his friends, not from his experiences. Reflecting on what he had just seen, his thoughts stray, "If only I could shag like that now, let alone in 50 years time!" The two old pensioners have by this time recovered and dressed themselves. Plucking up the courage, the man approaches the pensioner.

He says, "Sir, in all my life I have never seen anybody shag like that, and particularly at you age. What is the secret? Could you shag like that 50 years ago?"

The little old man replies, "Son, 50 years ago, that f*cking fence wasn't electrified."

SUBJECT: ST. PETER

A man appears before the pearly gates. "Have you ever done anything of particular merit?" St Peter asks.

"Well, I can think of one thing," the man offers. "Once I came upon a gang of bikers who were threatening a young woman. I directed them to leave her alone, but they wouldn't listen. So I approached the largest and most heavily tattooed biker."

"I smacked him on the head, kicked his bike over, ripped out his nose ring and threw it on the ground, and told him, 'Leave her alone now or you'll answer to me.'"

St Peter was impressed. "When did this happen?"

"A couple of minutes ago."

SUBJECT: SCIENTIFIC PHRASES

Scientific Phrases – What They Say and What They Mean

"It has long been known."
> I didn't look up the original reference.

"A definite trend is evident."
> These data are practically meaningless.

"While it has not been possible to provide definite answers to the questions."
> An unsuccessful experiment but I still hope to get it published.

"Three of the samples were chosen for detailed study."
> The other results didn't make any sense.

"Typical results are shown:"
> 1. This is the prettiest graph.
> 2. The best results are shown.

"These results will be in a subsequent report."
> I might get around to this sometime, if pushed/funded.

"In my experience."
> Once.

"In case after case."
> Twice.

"In a series of cases."
> Thrice.

"It is believed that."
> I think.

"It is generally believed that."
> A couple of others think so, too.

"Correct within an order of magnitude."
> Wrong

continued...

"According to statistical analysis."
> Rumour has it.

"A statistically-oriented projection of the significance of these findings."
> A wild guess.

"A careful analysis of obtainable data."
> Three pages of notes were obliterated when I knocked over a glass iced tea.

"It is clear that much additional work will be required before a complete understanding of this phenomenon occurs:"
> 1. I don't understand it.
> 2. I need more grant money.
> 3. I can get at least one more paper out of this.

"After additional study by my colleagues."
> They don't understand it either.

"Thanks are due to Joe Blotz for assistance with the experiment and to Cindy Adams for valuable discussions."
> Mr. Blotz did the work and Ms. Adams explained to me what it meant.

"A highly significant area for exploratory study."
> A totally useless topic selected by my committee.

"Handled with extreme care during the experiments."
> Not dropped on the floor.

"Presumably at longer times."
> I didn't take the time to find out.

"This paper will omit a review of the more recent literature in favour of."
> I don't know if anything has been written on this since my dissertation.

"Various authorities agree."
> I overheard this in the hall.

"It was observed that."
  One of my students noticed that

"No discussion would be complete without reference to the contributions of:"
  I need another footnote on this page.

"This research has left many questions unanswered."
  I didn't find anything of significance.

"This finding has not yet been incorporated into general theory."
  Perhaps my next graduate student will make
  sense of it.

"It is hoped that this study will stimulate further investigation in this field."
  I quit.

SUBJECT: POOR DAVE

Dave returned from the doctor's and told his wife Alma that bad news, he had been told, he only had 24 hours to live.

Wiping away her tears, he asked Alma to make love with him. Of course Alma agreed and they made passionate love.

Six hours later, Dave went to her again and said, "Honey, now I only have 18 hours left to live. Maybe we could make love again."

Alma agreed and again they made love.

Later, Dave was getting into bed when he realised he now only had eight hours of life left.

He touched Alma's shoulder and said, "Honey? Please? Just one more time before I die."

Alma agreed, then afterwards she rolled over and went to sleep.

Dave, however, heard the clock ticking in his head, and he tossed and turned until he was down to only four hours.

He tapped Alma on the shoulder to wake her up. "Honey, I only have four hours left! Could we...?

Alma sat up abruptly, turned to Dave and said, "Listen Dave, I have to get up in the morning! You don't."

SUBJECT: THE PASSENGER

One dismal rainy night, a taxi driver spotted an arm waving from the shadows of an alley halfway down the block. Even before he rolled to a stop at the curb, a figure leaped into the cab and slammed the door.

Checking his rear view mirror as he pulled away, he was startled to see a dripping wet, totally naked woman sitting in the back seat.

"Where to?" he stammered.

"Union Station," answered the woman.

"You got it," he said, taking another long glance in the mirror. The woman caught him staring at her and asked, "Just what the hell are you looking at, driver?"

The driver replied, "Well, ma'am, I can't help noticing that you're completely naked, and I was just wondering how you'll pay your fare?"

The woman spread her legs, put her feet up on the front seat, smiled at the driver and said, "Does this answer your question?"

Still looking in the mirror, the cabbie asked, "Got anything smaller?"

SUBJECT: PICK-UP LINES

- When does your centerfold come out?
- You're like Pringles - Once I pop you, I can't stop.
- Hey baby, can I tickle your belly button from the inside?
- Why don't you sit on my face and let me eat my way to your heart?

SUBJECT: HOW TO CALL THE POLICE

George Phillips of Meridian, Mississippi as going up to bed when his wife told him that he'd left the light on in the garden shed, which she could see from the bedroom window. George opened the back door to go turn off the light but saw that there were people in the shed stealing things.

He phoned the police, who asked, "Is someone in your house?" and he said, "No." Then they said that all patrols were busy, and that he should simply lock his door and an officer would be along when available.

George said, "Okay," hung up, counted to 30, and phoned the police again. "Hello, I just called you a few seconds ago because there were people in my shed. Well, you don't have to worry about them now cause I've just shot them all." Then he hung up.

Within five minutes three police cars, an armed response unit, and an ambulance showed up at the Phillips' residence. Of course, the police caught the burglars red handed.

One of the Policemen said to George, "I thought you said that you'd shot them!" George said, "I thought you said there was nobody available!"

SUBJECT: PRETTY BAD

This guy goes to see his doctor with a piece of lettuce poking out his backside. The doctor says, "That looks nasty."

The guy says, "Nasty, that's just the tip of the iceberg"

THE DOG
A man takes his bull mastiff to the vet and says, "Doc, I think my dog has a lazy eye."

The vet picks up the dog and stares into its eyes for a few minute before stating, "Yes, he does have a lazy eye. I'm going to have to put him down."

"Why," cried the distraught man, "Just because he has a lazy eye?!?!"

"No," replied the vet, "because he's really bloody heavy."

SUBJECT: PAN AM PILOTS, ARE LISTENING

The German air controllers at Frankfurt Airport are renowned as a short-tempered lot.

They not only expect one to know one's gate parking location, but how to get there without any assistance from them. So it was with some amusement that we (a Pan Am 747) listened to the following exchange between Frankfurt ground control and a British Airways 747, call sign, Speedbird 206:

Speedbird 206, "Frankfurt, Speedbird 206 clear of active runway."

Ground Control, "Speedbird 206. Taxi to gate Alpha One-Seven."

The BA 747 pulled onto the main taxiway and slowed to a stop.

Ground Control, "Speedbird, do you not know where you are going?"

Speedbird 206, "Stand by, Ground, I'm looking up our gate location now."

Ground Control (with arrogant impatience), "Speedbird 206, have you not been to Frankfurt before?"

Speedbird 206 (coolly), "Yes, twice in 1944 but it was dark and I didn't stop."

SUBJECT: THE LEAST OF HIS PROBLEMS

“I have good news and bad news,” the defence attorney told his client. “First the bad news. The blood test came back, and your DNA is an exact match with that found at the crime scene.”

“Oh, no!” cried the client. “What’s the good news?”

“Your cholesterol is only 4.0”

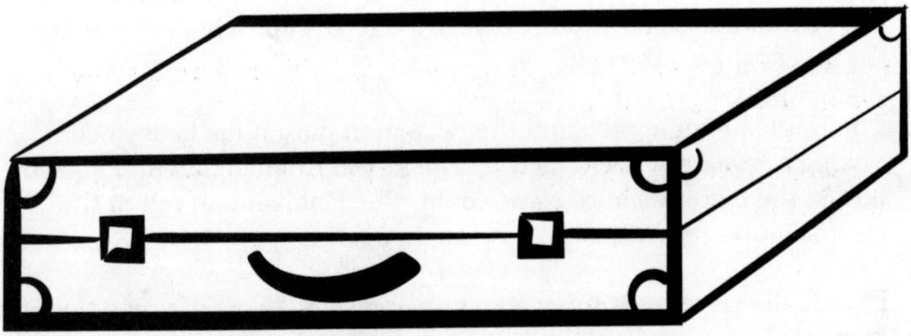

SUBJECT: PROBLEM SOLVING

The Scotsman and the Englishman lived next door to each other.

The Scotsman owned a hen and each morning would look in his garage, to pick up his hen's egg for breakfast.

One day he looked into his garden and saw the hen had laid its egg in the Englishman's garden. He was about to go and get the egg, when he saw his neighbor pick up the egg.

The Scotsman ran up to the Englishman and told him the egg was his because he owned the hen.

Of course the Englishman disagreed because the egg was laid on his property.

They argued for a while until finally the Scotsman said, "In my family we solve disputes by the following actions: I kick you in the testes, and see how long it takes you to get up; then you kick me in the testes and see how long it takes me to get up. Whoever gets up the quickest gets the egg."

The Englishman agreed and the Scotsman put on his heavy boots. Taking a few steps back, he then ran at the Englishman and kicked him in the testes as hard as he could. The Englishman fell to the ground clutching his groin, howling in agony.

Eventually the Englishman stood up and said, "Now it's may turn to kick you."

The Scotsman smiled and said, "Ye can keep the damn egg!!!"

SUBJECT: PSYCHOLOGICAL TEST

Read this question, come up with an answer, and then scroll down to the bottom for the result. This is not a trick question. It is as it reads. No one I know has gotten it right.

A woman, while at the funeral of her own mother, met this guy whom she did not know. She thought this guy was amazing. She believed him to be her dream and she fell in love with him right there but did not ask for his number and no matter how hard she tried she could not find him. A few days later she killed her sister.

Question: What is her motive in killing her sister?

Give this some thought before you answer.

(Scroll Down)

Answer:

She was hoping that the guy would appear at the funeral again.

If you answered this correctly, you think like a psychopath. This was a test by a famous American Psychologist used to test if one has the same mentality as a killer.

Many arrested serial killers took part in the test and answered the question correctly. If you didn't answer the question correctly – good for you.

SUBJECT: THE POPE COMES TO WASHINGTON

After getting all of the Pope's luggage loaded into the limousine, (and he doesn't travel light), the driver notices that the Pope is still standing on the curb. "Excuse me, Your Holiness," says the driver, "Would you please take your seat so we can leave?"

"Well, to tell you the truth," says the Pope, "they never let me drive at the Vatican, and I'd really like to drive today."

"I'm sorry but I cannot let you do that. I'd lose my job! And what if something should happen?" protests the driver, wishing he'd never gone to work that morning.

"There might be something extra in it for you," says the Pope.

Reluctantly, the driver gets in the back as the Pope climbs in behind the wheel. The driver quickly regrets his decision when, after exiting the airport, the Pontiff floors it, accelerating the limousine to 105 miles per hour.

"Please slow down, Your Holiness!!!" pleads the worried driver, but the Pope keeps the pedal to the metal until they hear sirens.

"Oh, dear God, I'm gonna lose my license," moans the driver.

The Pope pulls over and rolls down the window as the cop approaches, but the cop takes one look at him, goes back to his motorcycle, and gets on the radio.

"I need to talk to the Chief," he says to the dispatcher.

The Chief gets on the radio and the cop tells him that he's stopped a limousine going a hundred and five.

"So bust him," says the Chief.

"I don't think we want to do that, he's really important," said the cop.

The Chief exclaimed, "All the more reason."

"No, I mean really important," said the cop.

The Chief then asked, "Who ya got there, the Mayor?"

Cop, "Bigger."

Chief, "Governor?"

Cop, "Bigger."

"Well," said the Chief, "Who is it?"

Cop, "I think it's God!"

Chief, "What makes you think it's God?"

Cop, "He's got the F*cking Pope as a chauffeur!!"

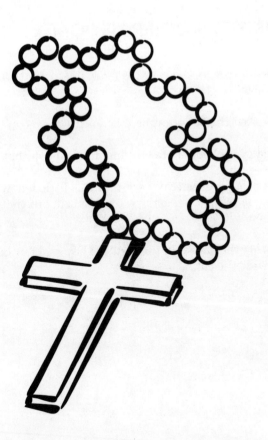

SUBJECT: PAIN

A man came home from watching a rugby match between Ireland and France.

He young son welcomed him home saying, "How was it, Dad?"

"It was terribly violent, son. In the break, the Irish skipper came off the field with a bruised testicle!"

"Oh, he must have been in such pain!"

"No, no, laddie. It belonged to one of the Frenchmen."

SUBJECT: POOR PUSSY CAT

A neighbour looked over his fence to see a little boy fillling a big hole.

He asked the boy what he was doing.

The boy replied, "I am burying my gold fish that died."

The neighbour felt very sad that this little fellow had to experience loss. He said, "I am sorry your fish died, but that is a large hole for a fish isn't it?"

Putting the shovel in the dirt, the boy said, "It has to be big, the fish is inside the cat."

SUBJECT: POST OFFICE INTERVIEW

A guy goes to the US Post Office to apply for a job.

The interviewer asks him, "Have you been in the service?"

"Yes," he says. "I was in Vietnam for three years."

The interviewer says, "That will give you extra points toward employment" and then asks, "Are you disabled in any way?

The guy says, "Yes 100 per cent... a mortar round exploded near me and blew my testicles off."

The interviewer tells the guy, "OK, I can hire you right now. The hours are from 8 a.m. to 4 p.m. You can start tomorrow. Come in at 10 a.m."

The guy is puzzled and says, "If the hours are from 8 a.m. to 4 p.m. then why do you want me to come in at 10 a.m.?"

"This is a government job" the interviewer says. "For the first two hours we stand around scratching our balls... no point in you coming in for that."

SUBJECT: THE POPE

The Pope dies and, naturally, goes to heaven. He's met by the reception committee, and after a whirlwind tour he is told that he can enjoy any of the myriad of recreations available.

He decides that he wants to read all of the ancient original text of the Holy Scriptures, so he spends the next eon or so learning languages. After becoming a linguistic master, he sits down in the library and begins to pour over every version of the Bible, working back from most recent 'Easy Reading' to the original script.

All of a sudden there is a scream in the library. The Angels come running in only to find the Pope huddled in his chair, crying to himself and muttering, "An 'R'! The scribes left out the 'R'." A particularly concerned Angel takes him aside, offering comfort, asks him what the problem is and what does he mean.

After collecting his wits, the Pope sobs again, "It's the letter 'R'. They left out the 'R'. The word was supposed to be CELEBRATE!"

SUBJECT: PROBLEMS - GOOD, BAD, UGLY

- Good – your wife is pregnant.
  Bad – she is expecting triplets.
  Ugly – you had a vasectomy five years ago.

- Good – your husband understands fashion.
  Bad – he is a cross-dresser.
  Ugly – he looks better than you.

SUBJECT: THE NEW PRIEST

A new priest was so nervous at his first mass, he could hardly speak After mass he asked the Monsignor how he had done. The Monsignor replied, "When I am worried about getting nervous on the pulpit, I put a glass of vodka next to the water glass."

So the next Sunday, he took the Monsignor's advice. At the beginning of the sermon, he got nervous and took a drink. He proceeded to talk up a storm. Upon his return to his office after mass, he found the following note on the door:

1. Sip the vodka, don't gulp.

2. There are ten commandments, not twelve.

3. There are twelve disciples, not ten.

4. Jesus was consecrated, not constipated.

5. Jacob wagered his donkey; he did not bet his ass.

6. We do not refer to Jesus Christ as, "The late J.C."

7. The Father, Son and the Holy Ghost are not referred to as, "Daddy, Junior and the Spook."

8. David slew Goliath; he did not kick the shit out of him.

9. When David was hit by a rock and knocked off his donkey, don't say, "He was stoned off his ass."

10. We do not refer to the cross as, "The Big T."

11. When Jesus broke the bread at the Last Supper he said, "Take this and eat it for it is my body..." He did not say, "Eat me."

12. The Virgin Mary is not called, "Mary with the Cherry."

13. The recommended grace before a meal is not, "Rub-A-Dub-Dub, Thanks for the grub, yeah God."

14. Next Sunday, there will be a taffy pulling contest at St. Peter's, not a Peter pulling contest at St. Taffy's.

SUBJECT: QUALITY OF LIFE

While I was watching the footy one weekend, my wife and I got into a conversation about life and death, and the need for leaving wills.

During the course of the conversation I told her that I never wanted to exist in a vegetative state, be dependent on some machine and take fluids from a bottle.

She got up, unplugged the TV and then to my amazement, threw out all my beer and scotch.

Sometimes it's tough being married to a smart arse.

SUBJECT: QUOTES

"Man: An animal [whose] chief occupation is extermination of other animals and his own species, which, however, multiplies with such insistent rapidity as to infest the whole habitable earth and Canada."
– Ambrose Bierce (1842 – disappearance in 1914)

"Woman: An animal... having a rudimentary susceptibility to domestication... The species is the most widely distributed of all beasts of prey... the woman is omnivorous and can be taught not to talk."
– Ambrose Bierce (1842 – disappearance in 1914)

"We need not worry so much about what man descends from – it's what he descends to that shames the human race."
– Mark Twain

SUBJECT: MALE QUESTIONS

Q: Why did God create women?
A: To carry semen from the bedroom to the bathroom.

Q: If a dove is the bird of peace, what is the bird of love?
A: Swallow.

Q: What should you do if your girlfriend starts smoking?
A: Slow down and use a lubricant.

SUBJECT: QUOTES FROM *HOLLYWOOD SQUARES*, I DON'T THINK I'VE SEEN BEFORE

Q. If you're going to make a parachute jump, at least how high should you be?

A. Charley Weaver: Three days of steady drinking should do it.

Q. True or False, a pea can last as long as 5,000 years.

A. George Gobel: Boy, it sure seems that way sometimes!

Q. According to Cosmopolitan, if you meet a stranger at a party and you think that he is attractive, is it okay to come out and ask him if he's married?

A. Rose Marie: No, wait until morning.

Q. Which of your five senses tends to diminish as you get older?

A. Charley Weaver: My sense of decency.

Q. In Hawaiian, does it take more than three words to say, "I Love You"?

A. Vincent Price: No, you can say it with a pineapple and a twenty.

Q. What are, 'Do It', 'I Can Help', and 'I Can't Get Enough'?

A. George Gobel: I don't know, but it's coming from the next apartment.

Q. Charley, you've just decided to grow strawberries. Are you going to get any during the first year?

A. Charley Weaver: Of course not, I'm too busy growing strawberries!

Q. In bowling, what's a perfect score?

A. Rose Marie: Ralph, the pin boy.

Q. It is considered in bad taste to discuss two subjects at nudist camps. One is politics, what is the other?

A. Paul Lynde: Tape measures.

Q. During a tornado, are you safer in the bedroom or in the closet?

A. Rose Marie: Unfortunately Peter, I'm always safe in the bedroom.

Q. Can boys join the Campfire Girls?

A. Marty Allen: Only after lights out.

Q. If you were pregnant for two years, what would you give birth to?

A. Paul Lynde: Whatever it is, it would never be afraid of the dark.

Q. According to Ann Landers, is there anything wrong with getting into the habit of kissing a lot of people?

A. Charley Weaver: It got me out of the Army.

Q. It is the most abused and neglected part of your body, what is it?

A. Paul Lynde: Mine may be abused, but it certainly isn't neglected.

Q. Back in the old days, when Great Grandpa put horseradish on his head, what was he trying to do?

A. George Gobel: Get it in his mouth.

Q. Who stays pregnant for a longer period of time, your wife or your elephant?

A. Paul Lynde: Who told you about my elephant?

SUBJECT: QANTAS PILOTS AND MECHANICS

After every flight, pilots fill out a form called a gripe sheet, which conveys to the mechanics problems encountered with the aircraft during the flight that need repair or correction.

The mechanics read and correct the problem, and then respond in writing on the lower half of the form what remedial action was taken, and the pilot reviews the gripe sheets before the next flight.

Never let it be said that ground crews and engineers lack a sense of humour. Here are some actual logged maintenance complaints and problems submitted by Qantas pilots and the solution recorded by maintenance engineers. By the way, Qantas is the only major airline that has never had an major accident.

(P = The problem logged by the pilot.)
(S = The solution, and action taken by the engineers.)

P: Left inside main tire almost needs replacement.
S: Almost replaced left inside main tire.

P: Test flight OK, except auto-land very rough.
S: Auto-land not installed on this aircraft.

P: Something loose in cockpit.
S: Something tightened in cockpit.

P: Dead bugs on windshield.
S: Live bugs on back order.

P: Evidence of leak on right main landing gear.
S: Evidence removed.

P: DME volume unbelievably loud.
S: DME volume set to more believable level.

P: Friction locks cause throttle levers to stick.
S: That's what they're there for.

P: IFF inoperative.
S: IFF always inoperative in OFF mode.

P: Suspected crack in windshield.
S: Suspect you're right.

P: Number three engine missing.
S: Engine found on right wing after brief search.

P: Aircraft handles funny.
S: Aircraft warned to straighten up, fly right, and be serious.

P: Target radar hums.
S: Reprogrammed target radar with lyrics.

P: Mouse in cockpit.
S: Cat installed.

P: Noise coming from under instrument panel. Sounds like a midget pounding on something with a hammer.
S: Took hammer away from midget.

SUBJECT: THE QUEENSLAND SUPPORTER

A man has great tickets for the State of Origin.

As he sits down, another man comes along and asks if anyone is sitting in the seat next to him. "No," he says, "the seat is empty."

This is incredible!" said the man. "Who in their right mind would have a seat like this for the State of Origin, the biggest sporting event in Australia, and not use it?"

He says, "Well, actually, the seat belongs to me. My wife was supposed to come with me, but she passed away. This is the first State of Origin we haven't been together since we got married."

"Oh... I'm sorry to hear that. That's terrible. But couldn't you find someone else, a friend or relative, or even a neighbour to take the seat?"

The man shakes his head. "No. They're all at the funeral."

SUBJECT: QUIET ONES

Mildred, the church gossip and self-appointed arbiter of the church's morals, kept sticking her nose into other people's business.

Several members were unappreciative of her activities, but feared her enough to maintain their silence. She made a mistake, however, when she accused George, a new member, of being an alcoholic after she saw his pick-up truck parked in front of the town's only bar one afternoon.

She commented to George and others that everyone seeing it there would know what he was doing. George, a man of few words, stared at her for a moment and just walked away.

He didn't explain, defend, or deny, he said nothing. Later that evening, George quietly parked his pick-up in front of Mildred's house... and left it there all night.

SUBJECT: QUOTE

"Women are like fine wine. They all start out fresh, fruity and intoxicating to the mind, and then turn full bodied with age until they go all sour and vinegary and give you a headache."

SUBJECT: RUSSIAN WOMAN

A Russian woman married an English gentleman and they lived happily ever after in London.

However, the poor lady was not very proficient in English, but did manage to communicate with her husband.

The real problem arose whenever she had to shop for groceries. One day, she went to the butcher and wanted to buy Chicken legs. She didn't know how to put forward her request, and in desperation, clucked like a chicken and lifted up her skirt to show her thighs. The butcher got the message, and gave her the chicken legs.

The next day, she needed to get chicken breasts. Again, she didn't know how to say it, and so she clucked like a chicken and unbuttoned her blouse to show the butcher her breasts! The butcher understood again, and gave her some chicken breasts.

The third day, the poor lady needed to buy sausages. Unable to find a way to communicate this, she brought her husband to the store...

(Please scroll down)

What are you thinking?

Helloooooooo, her husband speaks English!

Now get back to work...

SUBJECT: AUSTRALIAN RADIO
THIS IS ABSOLUTELY HILARIOUS !!!

Just imagine sitting in traffic on your way to work and hearing this.

Many Sydney folks DID hear this on the FOX FM morning show in Sydney. The DJs play a game where they award winners great prizes.

The game is called *Mate Match*. The DJs call someone at work and ask if they are married or seriously involved with someone. If the contestant answers, "Yes," he or she is then asked three random yet highly personal questions.

The person is also asked to divulge the name of their partner (with phone number) for verification. If their partner answers those same three questions correctly, they both win the prize. One particular game, however, several months ago made the City of Big Shoulders drop to its knees with laughter and is possibly the funniest thing I've heard yet.

Anyway, here's how it all went down:

DJ: "Hey! This is Ed on FOX FM. Have you ever heard of *Mate Match*?"
Contestant: (laughing) "Yes, I have."

DJ: "Great! Then you know we're giving away a trip to the Gold Coast if you win. What is your name? First only please."
Contestant: "Brian."

DJ: "Brian, are you married or what?"
Brian: "Yes."

DJ: "Yes? Does that mean you're married or you're what?"

Brian: (laughing nervously) "Yes, I am married."

DJ: "Thank you. Now, what is your wife's name? First only please."
Brian: "Sara."

continued...

DJ:	"Is Sara at work, Brian?"
Brian:	"She is gonna kill me."
DJ:	"Stay with me here, Brian! Is she at work?"
Brian:	(laughing) "Yes, she's at work."
DJ:	"Okay, first question – when was the last time you had sex?"
Brian:	"She is gonna kill me."
DJ:	"Brian! Stay with me here!"
Brian:	"About eight o'clock this morning."
DJ:	"'Atta boy, Brian."
Brian:	(laughing sheepishly) "Well..."
DJ:	"Question two – How long did it last?"
Brian:	"About ten minutes."
DJ:	"Wow! You really want that trip, huh? No one would ever have said that if a trip wasn't at stake."
Brian:	"Yeah, that trip sure would be nice."
DJ:	"Okay. Final question. Where did you have sex at eight o'clock this morning?"
Brian:	(laughing hard) "I, ummm, I, well..."
DJ:	"This sounds good, Brian. Where was it at?"
Brian:	"Not that it was all that great, but her Mum is staying with us for a couple of weeks..."
DJ:	"Uh huh..."
Brian:	"...and the Mother-in-law was in the shower at the time."
DJ:	"'Atta boy, Brian."
Brian:	"On the kitchen table."
DJ:	"Not that great?? That is more adventure than the previous hundred times I've done it. Okay folks, I will put Brian on hold, get this wife's work number and call her up. You listen to this."

Three minutes of commercials follow.

DJ:	"Okay audience, let's call Sarah, shall we?" (touch tones... ringing...)
Clerk:	"Kinkos."
DJ:	"Hey, is Sarah around there somewhere?"
Clerk:	"This is she."
DJ:	"Sarah, this is Ed with FOX FM. We are live on the air right now and I've been talking with Brian for a couple of hours now."
Sarah:	(laughing) "A couple of hours?"
DJ:	"Well, a while now. He is on the line with us. Brian knows not to give any answers away or you'll lose. Sooooooo... do you know the rules of *Mate Match*?"
Sarah:	"No."
DJ:	"Good!"
Brian:	(laughing)
Sarah:	(laughing) "Brian, what the hell are you up to?"
Brian:	(laughing) "Just answer his questions honestly, okay? Be completely honest."
DJ:	"Yeah, yeah, yeah. Sure. Now, I will ask you three questions, Sarah. If your answers match Brian's answers, then the both of you will be off to the Gold Coast for five days on us.
Sarah:	(laughing) "Yes."
DJ:	"Alright. When did you last have sex, Sarah?"
Sarah:	"Oh God, Brian... uh, this morning before Brian went to work."
DJ:	"What time?"
Sarah:	"Around eight this morning."
DJ:	"Very good. Next question. How long did it last?"
Sarah:	"12, 15 minutes maybe."

continued...

DJ:	"Hmmmm. That's close enough. I am sure she is trying to protect his manhood. We've got one last question, Sarah. You are one question away from a trip to the Gold Coast. Are you ready?"
Sarah:	(laughing) "Yes."
DJ:	"Where did you have it?"
Sarah:	"OH MY GOD, BRIAN!! You didn't tell them that, did you?"
Brian:	"Just tell him, honey."
DJ:	"What is bothering you so much, Sarah?"
Sarah:	"Well..."
DJ:	"Come on Sarah... where did you have it?"
Sarah:	"Up the arse..."

After a long pause, the DJ said: "Folks, we need to take station break"

SUBJECT: RULES ACCORDING TO WOMEN

The women always makes the rules.

The rules are subject to change at any time, without notification.

No man can possibly know the rules.

If the women suspects the man knows the rules, she must change some or all of the rules.

The woman is never wrong.

If the woman is wrong it is due to a misunderstanding, which was a direct result of something the man did or said.

The man must apologise immediately, for causing said misunderstanding.

The woman may change her mind at any time.

The man must never change his mind without express written consent from the woman.

The woman has every right to be angry and upset at any time.

The man must remain calm at all times, unless the woman wants him to be angry and upset.

The man is expected to mind read at all times.

The man who doesn't abide the rules can't 'take the heat', 'lacks backbone', and is a 'whimp'.

The woman is ready when she is ready.

The man must be ready at all times.

And if the woman has PMT, all the rules are null and void.

SUBJECT: QUITE CLEVER THIS...
REVENGE IS SWEET

A successful businessman flew to Vegas to gamble for the weekend. He lost the shirt off his back, and had nothing left but a quarter and the second half of his round trip ticket. If he could just get to the airport he could get himself home. So he went out to the front of the casino where there was a cab waiting.

He got in and explained his situation to the cabbie. He promised to send the driver money from home, he offered him his credit card numbers, his driver's license number, his address, etc. but to no avail. The cabbie said, "If you don't have $15, get the hell out of my cab!"

So the businessman was forced to hitchhike to the airport and barely made it in time to catch his flight.

One year later, the businessman, having worked long and hard to regain his financial success, returned to Vegas and this time he won big. Feeling pretty good about himself, he went out to the front of the casino to get a cab ride back to the airport. Well who should he see out there, at the end of a long line of cabs, but his old buddy who had refused to give him a ride when he was down on his luck.

The businessman thought for a moment about how he could make the guy pay for his lack of charity, and he hit on a plan. The businessman got in the first cab in the line.

"How much for a ride to the airport?" he asked.
"Fifteen dollars," came the reply.
"And how much for you to give me oral sex on the way?"
"What? Get the hell out of my cab."

The businessman got into the back of each cab in the long line and asked the same questions, with the same result. When he got to his old friend at the back of the line, he got in and asked, "How much for a ride to the airport?"

The cabbie replied, "Fifteen bucks."
The businessman said, "Okay," and off they went.

Then, as they drove slowly past the long line of cabs, the businessman gave a big smile and thumbs up to all the other drivers.

SUBJECT: YOUR AN EXTREME REDNECK IF...

You let your 14-year-old daughter smoke at the dinner table in front of her kids.

The blue book value of your truck goes up and down depending on how much gas is in it.

You've been married three times and still have the same in-laws.

You think a woman who is 'out of your league' bowls on a different night.

You wonder how service stations keep their toilets so clean.

Someone in your family died right after saying, "Hey, guys, watch this."

You think Dom Perignon is a Mafia leader.

Your wife's hairdo was once ruined by a ceiling fan.

Your junior prom offered day care.

You think the last words of the *Star-Spangled Banner* are, "Gentlemen, start your engines."

You lit a match in the bathroom and your house exploded right off its wheels.

The Halloween pumpkin on your porch has more teeth than your spouse.

You have to go outside to get something from the fridge.

One of your kids was born on a pool table.

You need one more hole punched in your card to get a freebie at the House of Tattoos.

You can't get married to your sweetheart because there's a law against it.

You think loading the dishwasher means getting your wife drunk.

SUBJECT: BRAND NEW 2006 EDITION OF 'YOU KNOW YOU'RE A REDNECK WHEN...'

You take your dog for a walk and you both use the same tree.

You can entertain yourself for more than 15 minutes with a fly swatter.

Your boat has not left the driveway in 15 years.

You burn your yard rather than mow it.

You think the *Nutcracker* is something you do off the high dive.

The Salvation Army declines your furniture.

You offer to give someone the shirt off your back and they don't want it.

You have the local taxidermist on speed dial.

You come back from the dump with more than you took there.

You keep a can of Raid on the kitchen table.

Your wife can climb a tree faster than your cat.

Your grandmother has, "ammo" on her Christmas list.

You keep flea and tick soap in the shower.

You've been involved in a custody fight over a hunting dog.

You go to the stock car races and don't need a program.

You know how many bales of hay your car will hold.

You have a rag for a gas cap.

Your house doesn't have curtains, but your truck does.

You wonder how service stations keep their toilets so clean.

You can spit without opening your mouth.

You consider your license plate personalised because your father made it.

Your lifetime goal is to own a fireworks stand.

You have a complete set of salad bowls and they all say, "Cool Whip" on the side.

The biggest city you've ever been to is Wal-Mart.

Your working TV sits on top of your non-working TV.

You've used your ironing board as a buffet table.

A tornado hits your neighbourhood and does a $100,000 worth of improvements.

You've used a toilet brush to scratch your back.

You missed your fifth grade graduation because you were on jury duty.

You think fast food is hitting a deer at 65 miles per hour.

And last, but not least...

Someone tells you that you've got something in your teeth, so you take them out to see what it is!

SUBJECT: RUGBY SHOCKER

I was sitting at a bar the other night, minding my own business and having a quiet beer.

After a while, this woman walked into the bar of such radiant and unparalleled beauty that everyone there turned in her direction and had their collective breath taken away.

Shortly after, I felt a presence beside me and turned to see this woman sitting next to me, staring at me. "Hello," she purred. "Uh, hi," I managed. "How are you," she continued. "Well," I replied.

Without warning, she took my hand and placed it on her bare thigh. "How's that feel," she asked. "Good," I admitted honestly and more than a little shocked. Confidently, she stated, "I'll bet it feels good. I'll bet it feels real good. I'll bet you haven't ever felt this good before."

"Well," I started, "actually I have. You see, when I was 18 I was selected for the New South Wales under 19 rugby league team to play Queensland as a curtain raiser to the first State-of-Origin match at Aussie Stadium. Running out in front of forty-odd thousand people was the most amazing experience of my life. Nothing could top that."

The woman was rather disgruntled at this so, liking a challenge, took my hand from her thigh and placed it inside her top.

"How's that feel," she demanded. "Great," I said too eagerly. "I'll bet it feels great," she teased. "I bet it feels really great. I bet you haven't felt this great before."

"Well, actually I have," I confessed. "During that game we were five points down with less than a minute to go. Queensland tried a clearing kick which I took on the full about twenty out from our line. I started up-field, stepping past the first few defenders, palming off the next couple, and out pacing two others. Coming to their last line of defence, I chipped over the top, re-gathered and sprinted around to score under the posts.

The crowd and my team mates went ballistic, the full-time siren sounded and I simply had to knock the conversion over from in front to win the game. Nothing will ever beat that feeling."

I could sense she was getting a tad peeved as she stood up, yanked my hand from her top, turned around and placed my hand on her rear end. "NOW TELL ME," she snapped, "HAVE YOU EVER FELT SUCH AN ASS!?!?"

"Yes I have. I missed the kick."

SUBJECT: RASTUS

Rastus and his son were working in the field one day and a plane flies by and the son gets all excited says, "Pa, Pa what's that?" Rastus says, "I don't rightly know son."

So they kept working and then a train goes by and again the son gets excited and points and says, "Pa, Pa what's that?" Rastus says, "I don't rightly know son."

So they kept on working and then a car goes by and the son shouts, "Pa, Pa what's that?" Rastus says, "I don't rightly know son."

After a while the son says, "Pa, I hope you don't mind me asking you all these questions?"

Rastus says, "That's OK son, that's how you learn."

SUBJECT: ROYAL COUPLE'S WEDDING NIGHT

As Camilla was making last minute preparations to walk down the aisle, she found that her shoes were missing. She was forced to borrow her sister's, which were a bit on the small side.

When the day's festivities were finally over, Charles and Camilla retired to their room, right next door to the Queen's and Prince Phillip's.

As soon as Charles and Camilla were inside their room, Camilla flopped on the bed and said, "Darling, please get these shoes off. My feet are killing me." The ever obedient Prince of Wales attacked the right shoe with vigour, but it was stuck fast.

"Harder!" Camilla yelled. "Harder!"

"I'm trying, darling!" The Prince yelled back. "It's just so bloody tight!"

"Come on! Give it all you've got!"

There was a big groan from the Prince, and then Camilla exclaimed, "There! That's it! Oh that feels good! Oh that feels SOOO good!"

In the bedroom next door, the Queen turned to Prince Phillip and said, "See? I told you, with a face like that she was still a virgin."

Back in the bridal suite, Charles was trying to pry off the left shoe.

"Oh, my God, darling! This one's even tighter!" exclaimed the heir to the throne.

At which Prince Phillip turned to the Queen and said, "That's my boy. Once a Navy man, always a Navy man!"

SUBJECT: RELIGIOUS DEVOTION

A Christian, a Moslem, and a Jewish man, all very pious, met at an inter faith congress and got to talking about the experiences that had lead to their religious devotion.

The Christian recounted being on a plane when it ran into a terrible storm over a remote wilderness area. "There was lightening and thunder all around us. The pilot told us to brace for the crash. I dropped to my knees and prayed to God to save us. Then for a thousand feet all around us the wind calmed and the rain stopped. We made it to the airport. And since then my faith has never wavered."

The Moslem then told of a terrifying incident on his pilgrimage to Mecca. "A tremendous sandstorm came up out of nowhere, and within minutes my camel and I were almost buried. Sure I was going to die, I prostrated myself toward Mecca and prayed to Allah to deliver me. And suddenly, for a thousand feet all around me, the swirling dust settled and I was able to make my way safely across the desert. Since then I have been the most devout of believers."

Nodding respectfully, the Jewish man then told his story. "One Sabbath I was walking back from the temple when I saw a huge sack of money just lying there at the edge of the road. It had clearly been abandoned, and I felt it was mine to take home. But obviously this would have been a violation of the Sabbath. So I dropped to my knees and prayed to Yahweh. And suddenly, for a thousand feet all around me, it was Tuesday."

SUBJECT: SHIPWRECKED

A man was washed up on a beach after a terrible shipwreck. Only a sheep and a sheepdog were washed up with him. After looking around, he realised that they were stranded on a deserted island.

After being there a while, he got into the habit of taking his two animal companions to the beach every evening to watch the sun set.

One particular evening, the sky was a fiery red with beautiful cirrus clouds, the breeze was warm and gentle a perfect night for romance.

As they sat there, the sheep started looking better and better to the lonely man. Soon, he leaned over to the sheep and put his arm around it.

But the sheepdog, ever protective of the sheep, growled fiercely until the man took his arm from around the sheep.

After that, the three of them continued to enjoy the sunsets together, but there was no more cuddling.

A few weeks passed by and, 'lo and behold, there was another shipwreck.

The only survivor was Hilary Clinton.

That evening, the man introduced Hilary to the evening beach ritual.

It was another beautiful evening red sky, cirrus clouds, a warm and gentle breeze perfect for a night of romance. Pretty soon, the man started to get 'those feelings' again.

He fought the urges as long as he could, but he finally gave in and leaned over to Hilary, cautiously, and whispered in her ear,

"Would you mind taking the dog for a walk?"

SUBJECT: STUN GUN... ONLY A GUY WOULD DO THIS

Pocket Taser Stun Gun, a great gift for the wife.

This as submitted by a guy who purchased his lovely wife a 'Pocket Taser' for their anniversary:

Last weekend I saw something at Larry's Pistol and Pawn Shop that sparked my interest. The occasion was our 22nd anniversary and I was looking for a little something extra for my wife Toni. What I came across was a 100,000 volt, pocket/purse sized Taser. The effects of the taser were suppose to be short lived, with no long term adverse affect on your assailant, allowing her adequate time to retreat to safety... WAY TOO COOL! Long story short, I bought the device and brought it home. I loaded two triple A batteries in the darn thing and pushed the button. Nothing! I was disappointed. I learned, however, that if I pushed the button AND pressed it against a metal surface at the same time, I'd get the blue arch of electricity darting back and forth between the prongs. Awesome!!! Unfortunately, I have yet to explain to Toni what that burn spot is on the face of her microwave.

Okay, so I was home alone with this new toy, thinking to myself that it couldn't be all that bad with only two triple A batteries, right?!!! There I sat in my recliner, my cat Gracie looking on intently (trusting little soul) while I was reading the directions and thinking that I really needed to try this thing out on a flesh and blood moving target. I must admit I thought about zapping Gracie (for a fraction of a second) and thought better of it. She is such a sweet cat. But, if I was going to give this thing to my wife to protect herself against a mugger, I did want some assurance that it would work as advertised. Am I wrong?

So, there I sat in a pair of shorts and a tank top with my reading glasses perched delicately on the bridge of my nose, directions in one hand, taser in another. The directions said that a one second burst would shock and disorient your assailant; a two second burst was supposed to cause muscle spasms and a major loss of bodily control; a three second burst would purportedly make your assailant flop on the ground like a fish out of water. Any burst longer than three seconds would be wasting the batteries.

All the while I'm looking at this little device measuring about five inches long, less than 3/4 inch in circumference, pretty cute really and loaded with two itsy, bitsy triple A batteries thinking to myself, "no possible way!" What happened next is almost beyond description, but I'll do my best...

I'm sitting there alone, Gracie looking on with her head cocked to one side as to say, "don't do it master," reasoning that a one second burst from such a tiny little 'ol thing couldn't hurt all that bad. I decided to give myself a one second burst just for the heck of it. I touched the prongs to my naked thigh, pushed the button, and OH MY GOSH, WEAPONS OF MASS DESTRUCTION @$%!@ *!!!

I'm pretty sure Jessie Ventura ran in through the side door, picked me up in the recliner, then body slammed us both on the carpet, over and over and over again. I vaguely recall waking up on my side in the fetal position, with tears in my eyes, body soaking wet, both nipples on fire, testicles nowhere to be found, with my left arm tucked under my body in the strangest position, and tingling in my legs. The cat was standing over me making meowing sounds I had never heard before, licking my face, undoubtedly thinking to herself, "do it again, do it again!"

Note: If you ever feel compelled to 'mug' yourself with a taser, one note of caution: there is no such thing as a one second burst when you zap yourself. You will not let go of that thing until it is dislodged from your hand by a violent thrashing about on the floor. A three second burst would be considered conservative.

SON OF A GUN that hurt like the dickens!!!

A minute or so later (I can't be sure, as time was a relative thing at that point), collected my wits (what little I had left), sat up and surveyed the landscape.

My bent reading glasses were on the mantel of the fireplace. How did they up get there??? My triceps, right thigh and both nipples were still twitching. My face felt like it had been shot up with Novocaine, and my bottom lip weighed 88 pounds. I'm still looking for my testicles!!

I'm offering a significant reward for their safe return.

SUBJECT: SCRIPTURE

The elderly lady having just arrived home from church services, was startled by an intruder. Having caught the young man in the act of robbing her home of its valuables and yelled, "Stop! Acts 2:38 (repent and be Baptised in the name of Jesus Christ so that your sins may be forgiven)."

The burglar stopped in his tracks. The woman calmly called the police and told them what she had done.

As the officer handcuffed the man, he asked the burglar, "Why did you just stand there? All the little old lady did was yell a scripture at you."

"Scripture?" replied the burglar.

"She said she had an axe and two 38s."

SUBJECT: THE TROUBLE WITH SEX

Usually everybody who had a dog called it Rover or Rex or Spot but I called mine 'Sex'.

Well, Sex turned out to be a very embarrassing name. One day while taking Sex for a walk he ran away from me and I spent hours looking for him. A policeman came along and asked me what I was doing in an alley at 2 a.m. I said, "I am looking for Sex." My case came up the next week.

One day I went down to the Town Hall to get a dog license for Sex. The clerk asked me what I wanted. I told him I wanted a license for Sex. He said, "I would like one too." When I told him it was for a dog the clerk said, "I don't care what she looks like." I said, "You don't understand. I have had Sex since I was five years old." The clerk, "By jove you must have been a very strong and virile boy."

When I decided to get married I told the minister that I wanted to have Sex at the wedding, but he told me to try and wait till after the ceremony. I said, "But Sex has played a big part in my life and my whole life revolves around Sex." I told him that every one at the wedding would enjoy having Sex there. The minister said, "I don't want to hear about your personal life and I shall not marry you in the church. My family are barred from the church. The next day we were married by a Justice of the Peace.

My wife and I took the dog on our honeymoon and when I checked into the motel, I told the Manager I wanted a room for my wife and a special room for Sex. He told me that every room in the motel was for sex. I said to him, "You don't understand, Sex keeps me awake at night." He said, "Me too."

When my wife and I separated, we went to court to fight for the custody of the dog. I said, "Your Honour, I had Sex before I was married," the Judge said, "Me too."

Well now I've been thrown in goal, married and divorced and had more darn trouble with that darn dog than ever I gambled for. Just the other day when I went for my fist session with the Psychiatrist he asked me what seemed to be the trouble, I replied that Sex had died and left my life and was like losing a best friend and It's lonely. The Doctor looked at me and said, "Mister, you and I know that sex isn't a mans best friend, so get yourself a dog."

SUBJECT: SMART ASS

Occasionally, airline attendants make an effort to make the in-flight safety lecture a bit more entertaining. Here are some real examples that have been heard or reported:

"As we prepare for takeoff, please make sure your tray tables and seat backs are fully upright in their most uncomfortable position."

"There may be 50 ways to leave your lover, but there are only four ways out of this aeroplane."

"Your seat cushions can be used for floatation, and in the event of an emergency water landing, please take them with our compliments."

"We do feature a smoking section on this flight. If you must smoke, contact a member of the flight crew and we will escort you to the wing of the aeroplane."

"Smoking in the lavatories is prohibited. Any person caught smoking in the lavatories will be asked to leave the plane immediately."

"Good morning. As we leave Dallas, it's warm, the sun is shining, and the birds are singing. We are going to Charlotte, where it's dark, windy and raining. Why in the world y'all wanna go there I really don't know."

Pilot, "Folks, we have reached our cruising altitude now, so I am going to switch the seat belt sign off. Feel free to move about as you wish, but please stay inside the plane till we land... it's a bit cold outside, and if you walk on the wings it affects the flight pattern."

And, after landing, "Thank you for flying Delta Business Express. We hope you enjoyed giving us the business as much as we enjoyed taking you for a ride."

As we waited just off the runway for another airliner to cross in front of us, some of the passengers were beginning to retrieve luggage from the overhead bins. The head steward announced on the intercom, "This aircraft is equipped with a video surveillance system that monitors the cabin during taxiing. Any passengers not remaining in their seats until the aircraft comes to a full and complete stop at the gate will be strip-searched as they leave the aircraft."

As the plane landed and was coming to a stop at Washington National, a lone voice comes over the loudspeaker, "Whoa, big fella... WHOA"

Here are a few heard from Northwest:
Should the cabin lose pressure, oxygen masks will drop from the overhead area. Please place the bag over your own mouth and nose before assisting children or adults acting like children."

"As you exit the plane, please make sure to gather all of your belongings. Anything left behind will be distributed evenly among the flight attendants. Please do not leave children or spouses."

And from the pilot during his welcome message:
"We are pleased to have some of the best flight attendants in the industry... Uunfortunately none of them are on this flight!"

SUBJECT: TAKING A SICKIE

Kung Chow called his boss and said, "Hey boss, I no come work today. I real sick. I got headache. Stomach ache. Leg Hurt. I no come work."

The boss says, "Kung Chow, I really need you today. When I feel sick like this, I go to my wife and tell her to give me sex. That makes me feel better and then I can go to work... You should try that."

Two hours later... Kung Chow calls again, "Boss, I do what you say and I feeling great! I be at work soon... You got nice house..."

SUBJECT: SIGN LANGUAGE ON THE CONSTRUCTION SITE

The construction worker on the third floor needed a handsaw.

He sees another worker on the first floor, and yells down to him, but he can't be heard so he starts to sign language. He points at his eye meaning 'I', points to his knee meaning 'need' and moves his hand back and forth in a handsaw motion.

The man on the first floor nodded his head, pulled down his pants and starts masturbating.

The man on the third floor gets so angry he runs down to the first floor and yells at his coworker, "What the hell is wrong with you dumbass? I said I needed a handsaw!!"

The other guy says, "I knew that, I was just trying to tell you I'm coming."

SUBJECT: SHORT STORY

In the human body, which organ is in charge?

All the organs of the body were having a meeting, trying to decide who was in charge.

The brain said, "I should be in charge, because I run all the body's systems, without me nothing would happen."

"I should be in charge," said the heart, "because I pump the blood and circulate the oxygen all over the body, so without me you'd all waste away."

"I should be in charge," said the stomach, "because I process the food that gives you energy."

"I should be in charge," said the rectum, "because I'm responsible for removals."

All the other body parts laughed at the rectum and insulted him, so as payback he shut down tight. Within a few days, the brain had a terrible headache and the stomach was bloated, and the blood was toxic. Eventually the other organs gave in. They all agreed that the rectum should be the boss.

The moral of the story is...

You don't have to be smart to be in charge... just an arsehole.

SUBJECT: STRANGE AND FUNNY SIGNS

On a Septic Tank Truck sign:
"We're No.1 in the No.2 business."

On a Plumbers truck:
"We repair what your husband fixed."

On a Plumbers truck:
"Don't sleep with a drip. Call your plumber."

Pizza Shop Slogan:
"Seven days without pizza makes one weak."

At a Tire Shop in Milwaukee:
"Invite us to your next blowout."

At a Towing company:
"We don't charge an arm and a leg. We want tows."

On an Electrician's truck:
"Let us remove your shorts."

In a Nonsmoking Area:
"If we see smoke, we will assume you are on fire and take appropriate action."

On a Taxidermist's window:
"We really know our stuff."

On a Fence:
"Salesmen welcome! Dog food is expensive."

At a Car Dealership:
"The best way to get back on your feet – miss a car payment."

Outside a Muffler Shop:
"No appointment necessary. We hear you coming."

In a Veterinary's waiting room:
"Be back in five minutes. Sit! Stay!"

SUBJECT: SOAP DISPENSER

Two priests are heading to the showers late one night.

They undress and get into the showers before realising there's no soap.

Father John remembers he has some soap in his room and goes back to get it, not bothering to dress.

He grabs a bar of soap in each hand and heads back to the showers. Halfway down the hall he sees three nuns coming towards him. Having nowhere to hide, he quickly freezes against the wall, pretending to be a statue.

The three nuns stop to look, commenting on how life like he looks. Suddenly the first nun reaches out and pulls on his manhood. Startled, he drops a bar of soap.

"Oh, look," the nun says, "it's a soap dispenser."

To test her theory the second nun reaches out and pulls on his manhood.

Sure enough, he drops the other bar of soap.

The third nun decides to give it a try.

She too pulls on his manhood, but nothing happens.

She gives it another tug, and a third and fourth.

Suddenly she exclaims, "Holy Mary, Mother of Jesus – Hand lotion too!!"

SUBJECT: THAT'S SLACK

A lady walks into a bar and sees a really good looking guy sitting
At the bar by himself. She goes over and asks him what he is
drinking.

"Magic Beer," he says.

She thinks he's a little crazy, so she walks around the bar, but after
realizing that there is no one else worth talking to, goes back to the
man sitting at the bar and says, "That isn't really Magic Beer, is it?"

"Yes, I'll show you."

He takes a drink of the beer, jumps out the window, flies around
The building three times and comes back in the window.

The lady can't believe it, "I bet you can't do that again."

He takes another drink of beer, jumps out the window, flies around
the building three times, and comes back in the window.

She is so amazed that she says she wants a Magic Beer. So, the guy
says to the bartender, "Give her one of what I'm having."

She gets her drink, takes a gulp of the beer, jumps out the window,
plummets 30 stories, breaks every bone in her body, and dies.

The bartender looks up at the guy and says, "You know,
Superman, you're a real arsehole when you're drunk."

SUBJECT: SHOCKERS... SOME OF THEM ARE GRRRREAT

Two TV antennas meet on a roof, fall in love and get married. The ceremony wasn't much, but the reception was excellent.

Two hydrogen atoms walk into a bar.
One says, "I've lost my electron."
The other says, "Are you sure?"
The first replies, "Yes, I'm positive..."

A jumper cable walks into a bar.
The bartender says, "I'll serve you, but don't start anything."

A man walks into a bar with a slab of asphalt under his arm and says, "A beer please, and one for the road."

Two cows standing next to each other in a field, Daisy says to Dolly, "I was artificially inseminated this morning." "I don't believe you," said Dolly. "It's true, no bull!" exclaimed Daisy.

An invisible man marries an invisible woman. The kids were nothing to look at either.

I went to buy some camouflage trousers the other day but I couldn't find any.

S

I went to the butcher's the other day and I bet him 50 bucks that he couldn't reach the meat off the top shelf. He said, "No, the steaks are too high."

A man woke up in a hospital after a serious accident.
He shouted, "Doctor, doctor, I can't feel my legs!"
The doctor replied, "I know you can't – I've cut off your arms!"

Two Eskimos sitting in a kayak were chilly, but when they lit a fire in the craft, it sank, proving that you can't have your kayak and heat it too.

Why do they bury dead farmers only one foot under?
So they can still get their hand out for a government payment.

SUBJECT: THE MOST FUNCTIONAL ENGLISH WORD

Well, it's shit... that's right, shit!
Shit may just be the most functional word in the English language.

With a little effort, you can get your shit together, find a place for your shit, or be asked to shit or get off the pot.

You can smoke shit, buy shit, sell shit, lose shit, find shit, forget shit, and tell others to eat shit and die.

Some people know their shit, while others can't tell the difference

You can find yourself in deep shit or be happier than a pig in shit.

Some music sounds like shit, things can look like shit, and there are times when you feel like shit.

You can have too much shit, not enough shit, the right shit, the wrong shit or a lot of weird shit.

And remember, once you know your shit, you don't need to know anything else!!

You could pass this along, if you give a shit, or not do so if you don't give a shit!

Well, Shit, it's time for me to go. Just wanted you to know that I do give a shit and hope you had a nice day, without a bunch of shit.

But, if you happened to catch a load of shit from some shit head... Well, Shit Happens!!!

SUBJECT: WHY I FIRED MY SECRETARY

Two weeks ago was my 45th birthday and I wasn't feeling too good that morning. I went to breakfast knowing my wife would be pleasant and say, "Happy Birthday!" and probably would have a present for me.

As it turned out, she didn't even say good morning, let alone any happy birthday. I thought, well, that's wives for you, the children will remember.

The kids came to breakfast and didn't say a word. So when I left for the office, I was feeling pretty low and despondent. As I walked into my office, my secretary, Janet, said, "Good morning, Boss. Happy Birthday." And I felt a little better that someone had remembered.

I worked until noon, then Janet knocked on my door and said, "You know, it's such a beautiful day outside, and it's your birthday, let's go to lunch, just you and me." I said, "Well, that's the best thing I've heard all day. Let's go!"

We went to lunch. We didn't go where we normally go, instead we went out to a private little place. We had two martinis and enjoyed lunch tremendously. On the way back to the office, she said, "You know, it's such a beautiful day, we don't need to go back to the office, do we?" I said, "No, I guess not." She said, "Let's stop by my apartment."

After arriving at her apartment she said, "Boss, if you don't mind, I think I'll go into the bedroom and slip into something more comfortable." She went into the bedroom and, in about six minutes, she came out carrying a huge birthday cake, followed by my wife, children, and dozens of our friends, all singing Happy Birthday.

And I just sat there... on the couch... naked...

SUBJECT: SAUSAGE

Larry and Bob wanted to go out drinking, but they only had two dollars between them.

Larry said, "Hang on, I have an idea." He went next door to the butcher's shop and spent the two dollars on one large sausage.

Bob said, "Are you crazy? Now we don't have any money left at all!"

Larry replied, "Don't worry – just follow me." They went into the pub where Larry immediately ordered two double shots of Jack Daniels.

Bob said, "Now you've lost it! Do you know how much trouble we will be in? We haven't got any money to pay for this!" Larry replied, with a smile, "Don't worry – I have a plan. Cheers!"

They downed their drinks. Larry said, "OK! I'll stick the sausage through my zipper and you get on your knees and put it in your mouth."

Said and done, the barman noticed them, went berserk, and threw them out. They continued this, bar after bar, getting more and more drunk, all for free. At the tenth bar, Bob said, "Larry – I don't think I can do this any more. My mouth is sore and my knees are killing me!"

Larry said, "How do you think I feel? I lost the sausage after the third pub..."

SUBJECT: SATAN

This guy dies and is sent to Hell.

Satan meets him and shows him the doors to three rooms and says he must choose one of the rooms to spend eternity in.

So Satan opens the first door. In the room there are people standing in shit up to their necks. The guy says, "No, please show me the next room."

Satan shows him the next room and this has people with shit up to their noses. And so he says no again.

Finally Satan shows him the third and final room. This time there are people in there with shit up to their knees drinking cups of tea and eating cakes. So the guy says I'll choose this room please. Satan says, "OK."

The guys is standing in there eating his cake and drinking his tea thinking, "Well it could be worse," when the door opens, Satan pops his head around, and says, "OK tea break's over. Back on your heads."

SUBJECT: STRANGE LAWS

1. In Lebanon, men are legally allowed to have sex with animals, but the animals must be female. Having sexual relations with a male animal is punishable by death. (Like THAT makes sense.)

2. In Bahrain, a male doctor may legally examine a woman's genitals, but is prohibited from looking directly at them during the examination. He may only see their reflection in a mirror.

3. Muslims are banned from looking at the genitals of a corpse. This also applies to undertakers, the sex organs of the deceased must be covered with a brick or piece of wood at all times. (A brick??)

4. The penalty for masturbation in Indonesia is decapitation. (Wonder which head?)

5. There are men in Guam whose full-time job is to travel the countryside and deflower young virgins, who pay them for the privilege of having sex for the first time... Reason: under Guam law, it is expressly forbidden for virgins to marry. (Let's just think for a minute, is there any job anywhere else in the world that even comes close to this?)

6. In Hong Kong, a betrayed wife is legally allowed to kill her adulterous husband, but may only do so with her bare hands. The husband's lover, on the other hand, may be killed in any manner desired. (Ah! Justice!)

7. Topless saleswomen are legal in Liverpool, England – but only in tropical fish stores. (But of course!)

8. In Cali, Colombia, a woman may only have sex with her husband, and the first time this happens, her mother must be in the room to witness the act. (Makes one shudder at the thought.)

9.   In Santa Cruz, Bolivia, it is illegal for a man to have sex with a woman and her daughter at the same time. (I gather this was a big enough problem that they had to pass this law?)

10.   In Maryland, it is illegal to sell condoms from vending machines with one exception: prophylactics may be dispensed from a vending machine only, "in places where alcoholic beverages are sold for consumption on the premises." (Is this a great country or what? Not as great as Guam!)

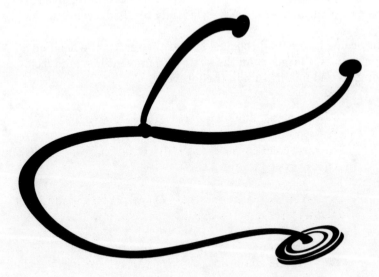

SUBJECT: SURPRISE

Several years ago the United States funded a study to determine why the head of a man's penis is larger than the shaft.

The study took two years and cost over $180,000. The results of the study concluded that the reason the head of a mans penis is larger than the shaft was to provide the man with more pleasure during sex.

After the results were published, Germany decided to conduct their own study on the same subject. They were convinced that the results of the US were incorrect. After three years of research and costs in excess of $250,000, they concluded that the head of a man's penis is larger than the shaft to provide the women with more pleasure during sex.

When the results of the German study were released, Australia decided to conduct their own study. The Aussies didn't trust the US or German studies. So after nearly three weeks of intensive research at a cost of around $75, the Aussie study reached a conclusion.

They came to the final conclusion that the reason the head on a man's penis is larger than the shaft is to prevent his hand from flying off and hitting him in the forehead.

SUBJECT: TRUE

This IS THE transcript of the true and actual radio conversation between a large military ship off the coast of a small country in 1998. Radio conversation released by the Chief of Naval Operations 10/01/01

Small Country: Please divert your course 15 degrees to the south, to avoid a collision.

Military Ship: Recommend you divert your course 15 degrees to the north to avoid collision.

Small Country: Negative. You will have to divert your course 15 degrees to the south to avoid a collision.

Military Ship: This is the Captain of a British Navy Ship. I say again divert YOUR course.

Small Country: Negative. I say again you will have to divert YOUR course.

Military Ship: THIS IS THE AIR CRAFT CARRIER AND THE LARGEST SHIP IN THE FLEET.
WE ARE ACCOMPANIED BY THREE DESTROYERS, THREE CRUISERS AND NUMEROUS SUPPORT VESSELS. I DEMAND THAT YOU CHANGE YOUR COURSE 15 DEGREES NORTH,
I SAY AGAIN, THAT IS 15 DEGREES NORTH, OR COUNTER MEASURES WILL BE UNDERTAKEN TO ENSURE THE SAFETY OF THIS SHIP.

Small Country: We are a lighthouse. Your call.

SUBJECT: THE TERRORIST

A man is standing in the urinal when he notices that a midget is watching him. Although the little fellow is staring at him intently, the guy doesn't really become uncomfortable until the midget drags a small ladder up next to him, climbs up, and proceeds to admire his privates up close.

"Wow" comments the midget, "those are the nicest balls I have ever seen!" Surprised, yet flattered, the man thanks the midget and starts to move away.

"Listen, I know this is a rather strange request," says the little fellow, "but I wonder if you would mind if I touch them?" Again the man is rather startled, but seeing no real harm in it, he complies with the request.

The midget reaches out, gets a tight grip on the mans balls, and says loudly, "Okay, hand me your wallet or I'll jump off the ladder."

SUBJECT: TAX

DEPARTMENT TAXATION
Notice of increase in Taxation Payments effective July 1, 2005.

TO ALL MALE TAXPAYERS
Gentleman.
The only thing the Federal Government has not yet taxed is your penis... mainly because 99 per cent of the time your penis is out of work, and the other 1 per cent it is in a hole.

However, it has two dependants, both of which are nuts. This notice is to advise that henceforth, as from 01/07/81 your penis will be taxed according to size, using the scale set out below to determine the category.

Please insert the information on page two, section F, line three, of your tax assessment form.

Yours Faithfully,

Jock Strapp
(Officer-in-charge of Penis Revenue)

SIZE CHART

10" to 12"	-----------------------------	Luxury Tax
7" to 9"	-----------------------------	Standard Tax
5 ½" to 6 ½"	-----------------------------	Pole Tax
4" to 5"	-----------------------------	Nuisance Tax

PLEASE NOTE:

Anyone under four inches is eligible for a refund.
Please do not request extensions.

MALES OVER 12" SHOULD FILE UNDER CAPITAL GAINS TAX.

SUBJECT: THE TEST

Three men who were lost in the forest were captured by cannibals.

The cannibal king told the prisoners that they could live if they pass a trial. The first step of the trial was to go to the forest and get ten pieces of the same kind of fruit. So all three men went separate ways to gather fruits.

The first one came back and said to the king, "I brought ten apples."

The king then explained the trial to him. "You have to shove the fruits up your butt without any expression on your face or you'll be eaten."

The first apple went in... but on the second one he winced out in pain, so he was killed.

The second one arrived and showed the king ten berries. When the king explained the trial to him he thought to himself that this should be easy. 1...2...3...4...5...6...7...8... and on the ninth berry he burst out in laughter and was killed.

The first guy and the second guy met in heaven. The first one asked, "Why did you laugh, you almost got away with it?"

The second one replied, "I couldn't help it, I saw the third guy coming with pineapples."

SUBJECT: THREE DEAD BODIES

Coroner's Report

Three dead bodies turn up at the mortuary, all with very big smiles on their faces.

The coroner calls in the police to tell them what has happened.

First body, "Frenchman, 60, died of heart failure while making love to his mistress. Hence the enormous smile, Inspector," says the Coroner.

Second body, "Scotsman, 25, won a thousand pounds on the lottery, spent it all on whisky. Died of alcohol poisoning, hence the smile."

The Inspector asked, "What of the third body?"

"Ah," says the coroner, "This is the most unusual one: Big Seamus O'Quinn from Donegal, age 30, struck by lightning."

"Why is he smiling then?" inquires the Inspector.

"Thought he was having his photo taken !!"

SUBJECT: TOWEL HEADS

Recently I received a warning about the use of 'Towel Heads' as politically incorrect term, so please note, we all need to be more sensitive in our choice of words.

I have been informed the Islamic terrorists, who hate our guts, bomb our subways and want to kill us, do not like to be called 'Towel Heads', since the item they wear on their heads is not actually a towel, but in fact, a small folded sheet.

Therefore, from this point forward, please refer to them as 'Little Sheet Heads'. Thank you for your support and compliance on this delicate matter.

SUBJECT: THE TRUCKIE

A big-rig operator stopped to pick up a female hitchhiker wearing really short shorts.

"Say, what's your name, Mister?" she drawled after climbing up into the truck.

"It's Snow... Roy Snow," he answered, "and what's yours?"

"Me, I'm June... June Hansen," she said.

After a short while she asked, "Hey, why do you keep sizing me up with those sidelong glances?"

"I was just imagining what it'd be like having eight inches of Snow in June."

SUBJECT: TRAINING

Memo to all employees:

In order to assure the highest levels of quality work and productivity from employees, it will be our policy to keep all employees well trained through our program of SPECIAL HIGH INTENSITY TRAINING (S.H.I.T.).

We are trying to give our employees more S.H.I.T. than anyone else. If you feel that you do not receive your share of S.H.I.T. on the course, please see your supervisor. You will be immediately placed at the top of the S.H.I.T. list, and our supervisors are especially skilled at seeing you get all the S.H.I.T. you can handle. Employees who don't take their S.H.I.T. will be placed in DEPARTMENTAL EMPLOYEE EVALUATION PROGRAMS (D.E.E.P. S.H.I.T.).

Those who fail to take D.E.E.P. S.H.I.T. seriously will have to go to EMPLOYEE ATTITUDE TRAINING (E.A.T. S.H.I.T.). Since our supervisors took S.H.I.T. before they were promoted, they don't have to take S.H.I.T. any more, and are all full of S.H.I.T. already.

If you are full of S.H.I.T., you may be interested in a job teaching others. We can add your name to our BASIC UNDERSTANDING LIST of LEADERS (B.U.L.L. S.H.I.T.). For employees who are intending to pursue a career in management and consulting, we will refer you to the department of MANAGERIAL OPERATIONAL RESEARCH EDUCATION (M.O.R.E. S.H.I.T.).

This course emphasizes how to manage M.O.R.E. S.H.I.T. If you have further questions, please direct them to our HEAD OF TEACHING, SPECIAL HIGH INTENSITY TRAINING (H.O.T. S.H.I.T.).
Thank you,
Boss In General, Special High Intensity Training
(B.I.G. S.H.I.T.)

Thank you for your time.
Sincerely,
The Director Under the Main Bureau of Super High Intensity Training. (The D.U.M.B. S.H.I.T.).

SUBJECT: TRUE STORY

On Thursday, 24 January 2002, Derek Guille broadcast this story on his afternoon program on ABC Radio.

In March 1999, a man living in Kandos (near Mudgee in NSW) received a bill for his as yet unused gas line stating that he owed $0.00. He ignored it and threw it away. In April he received another bill and threw that one away too.

The following month the gas company sent him a very nasty note stating that they were going to cancel his gas line if he didn't send them $0.00 by return mail. He called them, talked to them, and they said it was a computer error and they would take care of it.

The following month he decided that it was about time that he tried out the troublesome gas line figuring that if there was usage on the account it would put an end to this ridiculous predicament. However, when he went to use the gas, it had been cut off. He called the gas company who apologised for the computer error once again and said that they would take care of it.

The next day he got a bill for $0.00 stating that payment was now overdue.

Assuming that having spoken to them the previous day the latest bill was yet another mistake, he ignored it, trusting that the company would be as good as their word and sort the problem out. The next month he got a bill for $0.00. This bill also stated that he had ten days to pay his account or the company would have to take steps to recover the debt.

Finally, giving in, he thought he would beat the gas company at their own game and mailed them a cheque for $0.00. The computer duly processed his account and returned a statement to the effect that he now owed the gas company nothing at all.

A week later, the manager of the Mudgee branch of the Westpac Banking Corporation called our hapless friend and asked him what he was doing writing cheque for $0.00. After a lengthy explanation the bank manager replied that the $0.00 cheque had caused their cheque processing software to fail. The bank could therefore not process ANY cheques they had received from ANY of their customers that day because the cheque for $0.00 had caused the computer to crash.

The following month the man received a letter from the gas company claiming that his cheque had bounced and that he now owed them $0.00 and unless he sent a cheque by return mail they would take immediate steps to recover the debt. At this point, the man decided to file a debt harassment claim against the gas company. It took him nearly two hours to convince the clerks at the local courthouse that he was not joking.

They subsequently helped him in the drafting of statements which were considered substantive evidence of the aggravation and difficulties he had been forced to endure during this debacle.

The matter was heard in the Magistrate's Court in Mudgee and the outcome was this:

The gas company was ordered to:
1. Immediately rectify their computerised accounts system or Show Cause, within ten days, why the matter should not be referred to a higher court for consideration under Company Law.
2. Pay the bank dishonour fees incurred by the man.
3. Pay the bank dishonour fees incurred by all the Westpac clients whose cheques had been bounced on the day our friend's had been processed.
4. Pay the claimant's court costs, and
5. Pay the claimant a total of $1500 per month for the five month period March to July inclusive as compensation for the aggravation they had caused their client to suffer.

And all this over an amount of $0.00... Who employed these idiots??

SUBJECT: THE TAXI

A passenger in a taxi leaned forward to ask the driver a question and tapped him on the shoulder. The driver screamed, lost control of the cab, nearly hit a bus, drove up over the curb, and stopped just inches from a large plate glass window.

For a few moments everything was silent in the cab, and then the still shaking driver said, "I'm sorry, but you scared the daylights out of me."

The frightened passenger apologised to the driver, and said he didn't realize a mere tap on the shoulder could frighten him so much.

The driver replied, "No, no, I'm sorry. It's my entire fault. Today is my first day driving a cab...

I've been driving a hearse for the last 35 years"

SUBJECT: THREE LADIES

Three ladies all have separate boyfriends named Larry.

One evening while sharing a few drinks at the bar, one of the ladies suggests, "Lets name our Larry's after a soft drink, because I'm tired of getting my Larry mixed up with your Larry." The other two ladies agree.

The first lady speaks out, "Okay then, I'm gonna name my Larry 7-Up because he has seven inches and it's always up!" The three ladies hoot and holler, and then slap each other high fives.

Then the second says, "I'm gonna name my Larry Mountain Dew because he can mount and do me any day of the week." Again, the three ladies hoot and holler, and slap each other more high fives.

The third lady then says, "You know those two Larry's were good, but I'm gonna call my Larry Jack Daniels." The other two ladies shout in unison, "Jack Daniels? That's not a soft drink, that's hard Liquor."

The third lady replies, "that's my Larry.'

SUBJECT: UNIONS AT WORK

A dedicated Teamsters union worker was attending a convention in Las Vegas and decided to check out the local brothels. When he got to the first one, he asked the madam, "Is this a union house?"

"No," she replied, "I'm sorry it isn't."

"Well, if I pay you $100, what cut do the girls get?"

"The house gets $80 and the girls get $20," she answered.

Mightily offended at such unfair dealings, the union man stomped off down the street in search of a more equitable, hopefully unionised shop. His search continued until finally he reached a brothel where the madam responded, "Why yes sir, this is a union house. We observe all union rules."

The man asked, "And if I pay you $100, what cut do the girls get?"

"The girls get $80 and the house gets $20" she replied.

"That's more like it!" the union man said. He handed the madam $100, looked around the room and pointed to a stunningly attractive blonde. "I'd like her," he said.

"I'm sure you would, sir," said the madam.

Then she gestured to a 92-year-old woman in the corner,

"But Ethel here has 67 years seniority and she's next."

SUBJECT: VIRUSES

The George Bush Virus
Causes your computer to keep looking for viruses of mass destruction.

The John Kerry Virus
Stores data on both sides of the disk and causes little purple hearts to appear on screen.

The Clinton Virus
Gives you a permanent Hard drive with no memory.

The Al Gore Virus
Causes your computer to keep counting and re-counting.

The Bob Dole Virus
Makes a new hard drive out of an old floppy.

The Lewinsky Virus
Sucks all the memory out of your computer and then emails everyone about what it did.

The Arnold Schwarzenegger Virus
Terminates some files, leaves, but will be back.

The Mike Tyson Virus
Quits after two bytes.

The Oprah Winfrey Virus
Your 200 GB hard drive shrinks to 100 GB and then slowly expands to re-stabilise around 350 GB.

The Ellen Degeneres Virus
Disks can no longer be inserted.

The Prozac Virus
Totally screws up your RAM, but your processor doesn't care.

The Michael Jackson Virus
Only attacks minor files.

The Lorena Bobbitt Virus
Re-formats your hard drive into a 3.5 inch floppy and then discards it through Windows.

SUBJECT: VIAGRA

An elderly woman goes to the doctor and asks his help to revive her husband's sex drive.

"What about trying Viagra?" asks the doctor.

"Not a chance," says Mrs. Murphy. "He won't even take an aspirin for a headache."

"No problem," replies the doctor. "drop it into his coffee, he won't even taste it. Try it and come back in a week to let me know how you got on."

A week later Mrs. Murphy returns to the doctor and he inquires as to how things went.

"Oh it was terrible, just terrible doctor."

"What happened?" asks the doctor.

"Well I did as you advised and slipped it in his coffee. The effect was immediate. He jumped straight up, swept the cutlery off the table, at the same time ripping my clothes off and then proceeded to make passionate love to me on the table top. It was terrible."

"What was terrible?" said the doctor, "was the sex not good?"

"Oh no doctor, the sex was the best I've had in 25 years, but I'll never be able to show my face in McDonalds again."

SUBJECT: VET BILL

A woman brought a very limp duck into a veterinary surgeon.

As she lay her pet on the table, the vet pulled out his stethoscope and listened to the bird's chest. After a moment or two, the vet shook his head sadly, and said, "I'm so sorry, your pet has passed away."

The distressed owner wailed, "Are you sure?"

"Yes, I'm sure. The duck is dead," he replied.

How can you be so sure?" she protested. "I mean, you haven't done any testing on him or anything. He might just be in a coma or something."

The vet rolled his eyes, turned around and left the room. He returned a few moments later with a black Labrador Retriever. As the duck's owner looked on in amazement, the dog stood on his hind legs, put his front paws on the examination table and sniffed the duck from top to bottom.

He then looked at the vet with sad eyes and shook his head. The vet patted the dog and took it out, then returned a few moments later with a beautiful cat. The cat jumped up on the table and also sniffed the bird from its beak to its tail and back again. The cat sat back on its haunches, shook its head, meowed softly, jumped down and strolled out of the room.

The vet looked at the woman and said, "I'm sorry, but as I said, he is most definitely, 100 per cent certifiably, a dead duck." Then the vet turned to his computer terminal, hit a few keys, and produced a bill, which he handed to the woman.

The duck's owner, still in shock, took the bill. "$150!" she cried. "$150 just to tell me my duck is dead?!!"

The vet shrugged. "I'm sorry. If you'd taken my word for it, the bill would have been $20. But what with the Lab Report and the Cat Scan... it all adds up."

SUBJECT: VANESSA...

This is dedicated to everyone who ever attempted to get into regular work-out routine.

Dear Diary,
For my fortieth birthday this year, my wife (the dear) purchased a week of personal training at the local health club for me. Although I am still in great shape, since playing football 20 years ago, I decided it would be a very good idea to go ahead and give it a good try. Called the club and made my reservation with a personal trainer called Vanessa, who identified herself as a 24-year-old aerobics instructor and model for athletic clothing and swim wear. My wife seemed pleased with my enthusiasm to get started.

I was encouraged to keep a diary to chart my progress.

MONDAY
Started my day at 6 a.m.. Tough to get out of bed, but it was well worth it when I arrived at the health club to find Vanessa waiting for me. She was something of a Greek Goddess with blonde hair, dancing eyes, and dazzling white smile. WOOOOOOOO HOOOOOOOOO!!!!!!!!!!! Vanessa gave me tour and showed me the machines. She took my pulse after five minutes on the treadmill. She was alarmed that my pulse was so fast, but I attributed it to standing next to her in the Lycra aerobics outfit. I enjoyed watching the skilful way in which she conducted her aerobics class after my work-out today. Very inspiring, Vanessa was encouraging as I did my sit-ups, although my gut was aching from holding it in the whole time she was around. This is going to be a FANTASTIC week!!!!!!!!!!!!!!

TUESDAY
I drank a whole pot of coffee, but I finally made it out the door. Vanessa made me lie on my back and push a heavy bar in the air, and then she put weights on it! My legs were a little bit wobbly on the treadmill, but I made the full mile. Vanessa's rewarding smile made it all worthwhile. I fell GREAT!!! It's a whole new life for me.

WEDNESDAY
The only way I can brush me teeth is by lying on the toothbrush on the counter and moving my mouth back and forth over it. I believe a have a hernia in both pectorals. driving was okay as long as I didn't try to steer of stop. I parked on top of a GEO in the club parking lot.

Vanessa, was impatient with me, insisting that my screams were bothering the other club members. Her voice is a little to perky for early in the morning and when she scolds, she ahs this nasally whine that is VERY annoying. My chest hurts when I got on the treadmill, so Vanessa put me on the stair monster. Why the hell would anyone invent a machine to stimulate an activity rendered obsolete by elevators? Vanessa told me it would help me get in shape and enjoy life. She said some others shit too.

THURSDAY
Vanessa was waiting for me with her vampire-like teeth exposed as her thin cruel lips were pulled back in a full snarl. I couldn't help being half an hour late; it took me that long to tie my shoes. Vanessa took me to work out with dumbbells. When she was not looking, I ran and hid in the men's room. She sent Lars after me, then, as punishment, put me on the rowing machine, which I sank.

FRIDAY
I hate that bitch Vanessa more than any human being has ever hated any other human being in the history of the world. Stupid, Skinny, anaemic, little cheerleader. If there were a part of my body I could move without unbearable pain, I would beat her with it. Vanessa wanted to work on my triceps, but I don't have any triceps! And if you don't want dents in the floor, don't hand me the f*cking barbells or anything that weighs more than a sandwich. The treadmill flung me off and I landed on a health and nutrition teacher. Why couldn't it have been someone softer, like the drama coach or the choir director?

SATURDAY
Vanessa left message on my answering machine in her grating, shrilling voice wondering why I didn't show up today. Just hearing her made me want to smash the machine with my planner. However, I lacked the strength to even use the TV remote and wended up catching eleven straight hours of the Weather Channel.

SUNDAY
I'm having the church van pick me up for services today so I can go and thank GOD that this week is over. I will also pray that next year, my wife (the bitch), will choose a gift for me that is fun – like root canal or a vasectomy.

SUBJECT: THE VENTRILOQUIST

An Australian ventriloquist visiting New Zealand walks into a small village and sees a local sitting on his porch patting his dog.

He figures he'll have some fun, so he says to the Kiwi, "Can I talk to your dog?"

Villager: "The dog doesn't talk, you stupid git."
Ventriloquist: "Hello dog, how's it going mate?"
Dog: "Doin' alright."
Villager: (Look of extreme shock)
Ventriloquist: "Is this villager your owner?" (Pointing at the villager)
Dog: "Yep."
Ventriloquist: "How does he treat you?"
Dog: "Real good. He walks me twice a day, feeds me great food and takes me to the lake once a week to play."
Villager: (Look of disbelief) ...
Ventriloquist: "Mind if I talk to your horse?"
Villager: "Uh, the horse doesn't talk either, I think."
Ventriloquist: "Hey horse, how's it going?"
Horse: "Cool."
Villager: (Absolutely dumfounded)
Ventriloquist: "Is this your owner?" (Pointing to the villager)
Horse: "Yep."
Ventriloquist: "How does he treat you?"
Horse: "Pretty good, thanks for asking. He rides me regularly, brushes me down often and keeps me in the barn to protect me from the elements."
Villager: (Total look of amazement) ...
Ventriloquist: "Mind if I talk to your sheep?"
Villager: (In a panic) "The sheep's a liar."

SUBJECT: HOW TO DRIVE WOMEN CRAZY!!!

Disclaimer: Note that these techniques are only for humorous purposes and are not recommended for actual use. Use with an actual woman may cause serious injury or even death to the practitioner... and in fact, probably will. ;-)

1. Call her by the dog's name and then deny it.

2. Answer all her questions with a question, preferably one on a totally different subject.

3. Super glue the commode seat in the up position.

4. Shrink her jeans and when she overreacts because she thinks that she's gaining weight, give her a condescending smile and say that you prefer her with some meat on her bones.

5. Firmly refuse to ever ask for directions even if you find yourself in Georgia when your original destination was California.

6. Call her by your mother's name and then deny it.

7. Start a conversation with the dog in the middle of one with her.

8. Buy her power tools for Valentine's Day.

9. Never give her a straight answer.

10. Take up yodelling and practice a lot.

11. Quote Tim Allen to validate your position during arguments. (Argh! Argh! Argh!)

12. Leave the newspaper open to an ad for plastic surgery.

13. Pretend you forgot how to speak English.

14. Answer every question with "Yes, dear." (Use with caution as PMS is a valid murder defence in many states.)

SUBJECT: THE WITNESS

A blonde was summoned to court to appear as a witness in a lawsuit. The prosecutor opened his questioning with, "Where were you the night of August 24th?"

"Objection!" said the defence attorney. "Irrelevant!"

"Oh, that's okay," said the blonde from the witness stand. "I don't mind answering the question."

"I object!" the defence said again.

"No, really," said the blonde. "I'll answer."

The judge ruled, "If the witness insists on answering, there is no reason for the defence to object."

So the prosecutor repeated the question, "Where were you the night of August 24th?"

The blonde replied brightly, "I don't know!"

SUBJECT: WATER VERSES ALCOHOL

It has scientifically proven that if we drink one litre of water each day, at the end of the year we should have absorbed ore than one kilo of Escherichia Coli Bacteria found in the water that contains faeces. In other words, we are consuming one kilo of shit. However, we do not run that risk when drinking rum, gin, whiskey , beer, wine or together liquors because alcohol has to go through distillation process of boiling, filtering and fermentation.

It is my duty to communicate to all you people who are drinking water, to stop doing so. It has been scientifically proven that is unhealthy and bad for you.

THEREFORE. It is better to drink alcohol and talk shit, than to drink water and be full of it!!!!!!!!!!!!!!!

SUBJECT: A PHILANDER'S TALE

When Andy and Mandy first got married Andy said, "I am putting a box under the bed. You must promise never to look in it." In all their ten years of marriage, Mandy had never looked.

However, on the afternoon of their tenth anniversary, curiosity got the best of her and she lifted the lid and peeked inside. In the box were three empty beer cans and $81,874.25 in cash. She closed the box and put it back under the bed. Now that she knew what was in the box, she was doubly curious as to why there even was such a box with such contents.

That evening, they were out for a special anniversary dinner. After dinner, Mandy could no longer contain her curiosity and she confessed, saying, "I am so sorry. For all these years, I kept my promise and never looked into the box under our bed. However, today the temptation was too much and I gave in. But now I need to know, why do you keep the three beer cans in the box?"

Andy thought for a while and said, "I guess after all these years you deserve to know the truth. Whenever I was unfaithful to you, I put an empty beer can in the box under the bed to remind myself not to do it again." Mandy was shocked, but said, "I am very disappointed and saddened by your behaviour. However, since you are addicted to sex, I guess it does happen and I guess three times is not that bad considering your problem."

Andy thanked her for being so understanding. They hugged and made their peace. A little while later Mandy asked Andy, "So why do you have all that money in the box?" Andy answered, "Well, whenever the box filled up with empty cans, I took them to the recycling centre and redeemed them for cash."

SUBJECT: THE WAR

After the end of the Finnish war, a young female reporter from a British newspaper was sent to Finland to write an article about the soldiers homecoming. She had interviewed half a dozen, when she met Pekka on the street.

"Excuse me," she said, "but were you in the war?"

"Yah, I was in the infantry."

"Would you mind to answer a few questions for a newspaper article?"

"No, I wouldn't mind at all."

"When you came home, when the war was over, what was the first thing you did?"

"I f*cked me wife." Pekka said bluntly. The journalist went crimson, and tried desperately to change the subject.

"After that. I mean, what did you do after that?"

"I f*cked her again." he answered. If possible the journalist turned even more red, and got even more desperate to change the subject.

"Other than that! Uh – what did you do when you were finished with all that?"

"Then I un-strapped my skis and my heavy back pack."

SUBJECT: PRE WEDDING

I was happy. My girlfriend and I had been dating for over a year, and so we decided to get married.

My parents helped us in every way, my friends encouraged me, and my girlfriend? She was a dream! There was only one thing bothering me, very much indeed, and that one thing was her younger sister.

My prospective sister-in-law was twenty years of age, wore tight mini skirts and low cut blouses. She would regularly bend down when near me and I got many a pleasant view of her underwear.

It had to be deliberate. She never did it when she was near anyone else. One day little sister called and asked me to come over to check the wedding invitations. She was alone when I arrived. She whispered to me that soon I was to be married, and she had feelings and desires for me that she couldn't overcome and didn't really want to overcome.

She told me that she wanted to make love to me just once before I got married and committed my life to her sister. I was in total shock and couldn't say a word.

She said, "I'm going upstairs to my bedroom, and if you want to go ahead with it just come up and get me." I was stunned. I was frozen in shock as watched her go up the stairs. When she reached the top she pulled down her panties and threw them down the stairs at me.

I stood there for a moment, then turned and went straight to the front door. I opened the door and stepped out of the house. I walked straight towards my car. My future father-in-law was standing outside.

With tears in his eyes he hugged me and said, "We are very happy that you have passed our little test. We couldn't ask for a better man for our daughter. Welcome to the family.

"The moral of this story is: Always keep your condoms in your car."

SUBJECT: WOMAN

A woman, standing nude, looks in the bedroom mirror and says to her husband, "I look horrible, I feel fat and ugly – pay me a compliment."

The husband replies, "your eyesight is perfect."

SUBJECT: WISE, WORDS FOR MEN

1. How about asking your mother to spend the holidays with us?

2. Go ahead, eat the last piece of caramel pie, I hate skinny women.

3. We could have a great night at home, with nibblies and romance movies.

4. There's nothing on TV but football games, lets go shopping.

5. Who wants to play golf when I can get to see how good the lawn looks freshly mowed.

6. You know Pam Anderson just doesn't seem to have the brain power that I find so attractive in a woman.

SUBJECT: MRS. WARD

The phone rings. The lady of house answers, "Hello"

"Mrs. Ward please."

"Speaking."

"Mrs. Ward, this is Doctor Jones at the medical testing laboratory. When your Doctor sent your husband's samples to the lab, the samples from another Mr. Ward were sent as well, and now were uncertain as to which ones are your husbands. Frankly, it is either bad or terrible."

"What do you mean?" Mrs. Ward asks.

"Well one Mr. Ward has tested positive to Alzheimer's disease and the other Mr. Ward to AIDS. We can't tell which your husband's is."

"That's terrible! Can't we just do the test over?" questions Mrs. Ward.

"Normally, yes. But Medicare won't pay for these expensive tests more than once."

"And? What the hell am I supposed to do now?" she enquires very upset.

"The people at Medicare recommended that you drop your husband off in the middle of town. If he finds his way home, don't sleep with him."

SUBJECT: WHAT HAPPENED IN TEXAS…

The cowboy rode into town and stopped at the saloon for a drink.

Unfortunately, the locals always had a habit of picking on strangers, which he was. When he finished his drink, he found his horse had been stolen. Going back into the bar, handily flipped his gun into the air, caught it above his head without even looking and fired a shot into the ceiling.

"Which one of you side winders stole my horse?" he yelled with surprising forcefulness. No one answered. "Alright I'm gonna have a beer, and if my horse ain't back outside by the time I finish, I'm gonna have to do what I dun in Texas! And I don't want to have to do, what I dun in Texas!"

Some of the locals shifted restlessly. The man, true to his word, had another beer, walked outside, and his horse has been returned to the post.

He saddled up and started to ride out of town. The bartender wandered out of the bar and asked, "Say partner, before you go… what happened in Texas?"

The cowboy turned back and said, "I had to walk home."

THE OFFICE INBOX JOKE BOOK – JOKES FOR HIM